All

**SHAUN BYRNE
& NICK TESAR**

Day

**LOW (AND NO)
ALCOHOL MAGIC**

Cocktails

Hardie Grant

BOOKS

All Day Cocktails is more than your average cocktail book. It's a small step towards sustainability via flavour-packed, low- and no-alcohol drinks. This is something that Nick and I are incredibly passionate about, and that we've been focusing on behind the bar for years.

We often get asked why we make low- and no-alcohol cocktails. The simple answer is that there's more demand for them as people make positive lifestyle changes. Also, you can drink more of them and still remain level-headed. It definitely throws up some exciting challenges; you really have to get creative devising and using ingredients you wouldn't usually see in mixed drinks. Here, we've put what we have learned and created into print so that you can mix your own low- and no-alcohol cocktails at home.

The pages that follow explore a variety of fruits, vegetables, herbs and nuts, showing you how to prep them for cocktails (in fact, these 'prep' recipes are so versatile, we're sure you'll find myriad culinary uses for them; and there are even a few punch recipes to try) – and then mix the drinks. It's all about using what you have on hand to make the most of what's in season, and this book shows you when each variety is at its peak.

Whether you pick the ingredients from your garden or buy them from a farmers' market, whether you're a bar nerd or a beginner, this book is for you. We cover bar equipment and techniques (page 12) with a focus on hacks for the everyday kitchen. We give you basic recipes for common cocktail ingredients (page 211), along with tips that Nick and I have developed working behind bars for most of our lives.

We've also included our musings on sustainability (page 6) and why it's important to consider the environmental impacts of your cocktail preparation. Part of this is about using local ingredients, so you'll even find a handy table to help you source locally made alcohol (page 10) for your next cocktail-making session. One last note on this: while we are cocktail experts, we're only scratching the surface when it comes to sustainability. We hope this book encourages you to broaden your understanding of sustainable drinking, and to make small, positive changes to the way you buy and use ingredients.

Finally, a note on the word 'mocktails': we're not fans of it and we're not the only ones. The word itself actually mocks non-alcoholic beverages! While cocktails have classically contained alcohol, we don't believe they need to. No-alcohol cocktails can be just as, if not more, delicious than their boozy counterparts. Let us ditch the word mocktails in favour of cocktails and view all mixed drinks in the same light. Mocktails are dead, long live cocktails!

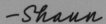

Notes on using this book

 Throughout you will notice this water-drop icon. This indicates that the recipe is alcohol-free.

Each cocktail recipe makes one drink, unless otherwise noted.

This book uses 20 ml (¾ fl oz) tablespoons; if you are using a 15 ml (½ fl oz) tablespoon, be generous with your tablespoon measurements.

Sustainability

Sustainability is a hot-button issue (and so it should be), with more and more people and businesses looking closely at their environmental footprint. Some progress has been made, such as a reduction in the use of plastic straws and the advent of reusable coffee cups. But long-term sustainability goes far beyond this, and must be actively pursued to create meaningful change.

Living sustainably is not always convenient. Contributing to waste reduction and making mindful buying decisions does call for extra effort. Nick and I are passionate about continually evaluating what we do and actively working towards positive change. We agree that living sustainably is a choice that must be consciously made, and it is a very worthwhile – even essential – one. However, the journey towards sustainability can be fraught with personal, environmental and economic challenges. If you have loads of time and money, we encourage you to go all out. But even small gestures are meaningful; it's their combined effect that contributes towards the greater good.

Here we invite you to consider how you can live more sustainably. Some suggestions may be achievable for you and some may not, but we do hope that you learn a thing or two and are inspired to implement some of the techniques.

Local & seasonal

Buy in season and, where possible, directly from the producer

Instead of heading to the supermarket for bland, out-of-season fruit from the other side of the world, have a wander through farmers' markets to see what's in season. This fruit will be more fresh and flavoursome than the glossy supermarket produce, which is often gassed and waxed to extend its shelf life. As well, local produce is more sustainable because it hasn't been cool-stored for months on end. Eating seasonally also has the added benefit of being cheaper, so it's win-win.

Buying sustainable, local produce goes far beyond just fruit. What about the liquor in your cocktails? Sure, you can buy gin made in London, or whisky from Scotland, but you can also buy local spirits that are just as good as the big-name brands. Supporting local businesses also helps to boost your local economy and reduces the environmental impact of imported products. If you must drink Champagne, try to limit your consumption and challenge yourself to try something new in its place, such as a local sparkling wine.

On page 10, you'll find suggested brands for each category mentioned in the book. While it's not an exhaustive list, it is a good guide to what's produced near you. We have focused on Europe, Australia and North America, but wherever you are in the world there is a surge in craft distillation.

Make use of a glut of fruit by preserving your produce

Making jams, ferments, pickles, chutneys, relishes and jellies, as well as air- or oven-drying your fruit, are great ways to preserve your harvest. A bunch of the recipes in this book show you how. If you still can't use it all, package up leftover fruit and gift it to friends, family and neighbours.

Social responsibility

We must all play our part in achieving sustainability. It's easy to get caught up in thinking that sustainability is an issue that only affects our environment but, at the very core, it affects us personally too. Sustaining ourselves and our health is of the utmost importance.

As we write this book, people are looking towards lower alcohol consumption to improve and sustain their health. Less alcohol also equates to less drink driving, fewer road accidents and less alcohol-fuelled violence. It is a great example of how we can use our personal agency to work towards a healthier, safer and more sustainable future.

Consider who you buy your products from and what their values are

What effect do they have on the environment around them? Do they use child labour? Do they dump harmful substances into waterways? How do they treat their workers? A good place to start is a brand's website. Accountable, ethically minded brands will be happy to share this information and answer questions.

Don't judge produce by its appearance

Just because a piece of fruit isn't uniformly shaped, it doesn't mean it isn't delicious. Not much in nature grows in a perfect shape – even us – and I encourage you to consider what intervention has taken place to make pristine, symmetrical fruit look that way. Unfortunately supermarkets impose strict standards on what their produce looks like, and farmers must conform to make a living. In the process a lot of rejected produce goes to waste, and farmers are unable to sell perfectly good fruit. Seek out your local farmers' market for these misshapen delights, and contribute to waste reduction at the same time.

Waste

These days, there is a lot of packaging around our fresh produce. Some of this is government-mandated plastic tamper-proof sealing, but much of it is unnecessary. Do your tomatoes really need to come on a polystyrene tray wrapped in plastic? And do your onions really need their own handy bag? Probably not. Most of this packaging isn't reusable and ends up in landfill, where it will sit for many years.

Single-use plastic straws are another contentious item but, thankfully, most good bars no longer offer them. In fact, they are being replaced with sustainable options, such as metal, paper, bamboo and even wheat straws.

Coffee cups are a hot point too, and it is great that more people are using reusable cups to get their caffeine fix. I would suggest you take it even further, though, and use your coffee break to slow down, relax and enjoy a coffee and good conversation in your favourite cafe with a friend or co-worker.

Reduce, reuse and recycle

We were taught this at school, but how many of us abide by it as adults? The order of the words is important too. Reducing your purchases limits the amount you need to reuse and recycle in the first place. Before you head out for your weekly shop, make a list of exactly what you need for that week and don't be tempted to put extraneous things in the trolley that will only be wasted.

Reusing your items, whether that's food in the form of leftovers or furniture that you can upcycle, is the next step to reducing waste. Take a look on the internet for some ideas for reusing many of your household products, especially plastics. You'll be surprised at what you can find. Egg-carton seedling trays, anyone?

Recycling should be the last thing we do, and only if items cannot be reduced or repurposed instead. This is because, even with the best will in the world, much of what we 'recycle' doesn't get recycled at all. It gets dumped in landfill where, under a pile of other rubbish, it does not receive enough light to adequately break down. So, before you give yourself a pat on the back for being a good recycler, look at what else you can do first.

Consider how you might use your leftovers

Think about how your offcuts might be repurposed. What about your strawberry tops or mint stems? These usually discarded parts actually contain a lot of flavour and can be used in secondary recipes. A number of recipes in this book use less desirable parts to make cordials, kefirs and vinegars (for example, see pages 25, 47, 73 and 173).

Compost your leftovers

If you can't repurpose your offcuts, compost them. Don't fear composting – it's actually quite easy. I was a little intimidated until my sister shared a bit of advice with me: for every bit of green waste you compost, such as food scraps, you need to add a bit of a brown waste, such as shredded paper, mulch or cardboard. This helps to keep your compost in balance. Easy!

The cost of sustainability

To compound matters further, we need to take the sustainability of sustainability into account. If a change can't be permanent, then it isn't sustainable. Here are a few personal factors you need to consider.

Consider the impact on your time

While something might be more sustainable for the environment, it might not be sustainable for you. This is one aspect of the sustainability conversation that is often ignored and can fly in the face of all the positive changes we have outlined. Doing what you can with what you've got is our advice here. For example, it may be environmentally sustainable to make passata from tomatoes grown in your backyard, but what impact does this have on your time? Preparing passata probably isn't viable if you don't enjoy tending to tomatoes and harvesting them. Maybe reducing your plastic waste or starting a compost heap is more achievable.

Live within your means when trying to make positive changes

While it is all good and well to advise people to be more sustainable, we cannot ignore that some of these measures cost money. Locally produced, hand-crafted products are, because of the passion and care that goes into making them, typically more expensive. If you were to only buy ethical, seasonal and local products, would that be sustainable for your bank account? If not, then look at what you can do, even if that's as simple as swapping out those endless plastic bottles of sparkling water for a soda maker instead.

Drink local

Category	Australia	Europe	North America
Amaretto	Marionette	Varnelli Disaranno	Oak City
Anise liqueur	Distillery Botanica Hurdle Creek Kangaroo Island Spirits	La Clandestine Jean Boyer Pernod	St George Copper & Kings
Apple brandy	Charles Oats Adelaide Hill Distillery Belgrove	Victor Gontier Eric Bordelet Roger Groult	Laird's Cornelius Santa Fe
Apple liqueur	Belgrove Castleglen	Massenez Vedrene	Leopold Bros
Apricot brandy liqueur	Marionette	Giffard Marie Brizzard	Charles Jacquin et Cie
Aquavit	Never Never	Linie Arcus	Vikre's Distilling Long Road Distilling
Aromatic bitters	Mr Bitters Batch Australian Bitters Company	Dr Adam Almegirab's Bob's Bitter Truth	Angostura Peychaud's Bittermans
Bitter liqueur	Applewood Adelaide Hills Ounce	Campari Aperol Gran Classico	St George Leopold Bros New Deal Distillery
Brandy	St Agnes Sullivans Cove Hardy's	Francois Voyer H By Hine Dalord	Germain-Robin Millard Fillmore Frisco
Curaçao	Marionette	Pierre Ferand Bertrand	Leopold Bros
Dark rum	Hoochery Bundaberg Beenleigh	BOWS Distillerie Arehucas O'Baptiste	Ipswich Distillery Richland Distilling Lyon Distilling Co
Dry fortified wine	Pennyweight Pfeiffer Seppeltsfield	Equipo Navasos Delgado Zuleta Tio Pepe's	Quady Joseph Filippi Pleasant Valley Wine Company
Dry vermouth	Maidenii Castagna Regal Rogue	Dolin Noilly Pratt Belsazar	Vya Ransom Imbue
Gin	Anther Melbourne Gin Company Four Pillars	East London Sipsmith Citadelle	St George Aviation Deaths Door Spirits

Category	Australia	Europe	North America
Gin liqueur	Brogans Way McHenry Brookie's	Hayman's Edinbrough Plymouth	Greenhook Spirit Works Distillery
Grain whisky	Starward	Teeling Jameson	Hudson Koval

Herbal liqueur	Original Spirits
	  (EXQ Harvest)
	Tamborine Mountain
	  Distillery
		Chartreuse
		Jagermeister
			Bittermans
			Lepold Bros

Hydrosol (floral water)	Brunswick Aces ALTD Spirits	Seedlip Ceder's Stryyk	Arkay
Peated whisky	Belgrove Distillery Limeburners Bakery Hill Distillery	Zuidam Talisker Lagavulin	Westland Distillery Woodford Reserve High West

Quinquina	Maidenii
	Turkey Flat Vineyards
		Lillet Blanc
		Saint Raphael
			Dubonnet (North
			  American–made
			  version)

Rye whisky	Belgrove Limeburners	Zuidam Stauning	Whistle Pig Rittenhouse Few
Sake	Sun Masamune	Kenshosake	Blue Currant
Sweet fortified wine	Simao & Co Stanton & Kileen Chambers	Fonseca Niepoort Romate	Charbay Winery & Distillery Anaba Wines Robeldo Family Winery
Sweet vermouth	Maidenii Regal Rogue Adelaide Hills	Cocchi Carpano Dolin	Atsby Interrobang Harris Bridge
White rum/sugar cane	Husk Distillers Archie Rose Brix Distillers	Pott Arehucas O' Baptiste	Bayou Montanya Noble Experiment Distillery

Everyday equipment, techniques & hacks

Having a complete bartending kit is fantastic, but putting it together can be an expensive exercise. Luckily you can use everyday kitchen items instead. Here are some equipment substitutes and techniques so you can easily replicate cocktail recipes at home.

Bar spoon

While the ability to twirl a bar spoon between your fingers is a fantastically elegant flair, a regular dessert spoon will work just fine. Angle it so that the back of the spoon is up against the inside of the glass or whatever vessel you are mixing your drinks in. This will allow it to slide easily around the glass as you stir and ensure there aren't any stray cubes of ice and splashes of drink flying everywhere. Alternatively, for longer reach, use a metal skewer.

Egg white

If you are not the kind of household that goes through egg yolks, or are of a vegan persuasion, do not despair; there are other ways to achieve that foamy texture in your cocktails. The first option is to drain the liquid (otherwise known as aquafaba) from your next tin of chickpeas. This liquid can then be used in 15 ml (½ fl oz) portions for individual cocktails. There are also products coming out that are made from bark extract, such as the *Quillaja saponaria*, or soap bark tree. A couple of drops will have the same effect. You'll find it at the best cocktail supply stores.

Fermenting

The basic theory of fermentation is that yeast will consume sugars, converting them into heat, ethanol (alcohol) and carbon dioxide (bubbles or gas). So, to have fermentation, both yeast and sugars must be present.

With fermentation, it is very important to make sure that the vessels and equipment being used are cleaned properly. Fermentation involves cultivating the microorganisms found in the air and on the fruits, so it is imperative to avoid any cross-contamination from leftover residue that might be on your kitchen utensils.

Temperature is also a contributing factor to fermentation. A rise in temperature will accelerate the process; a drop will slow it. For this reason, monitoring is important. This is also why, when the fermentation has reached the desired point, you must refrigerate your ferment to arrest the fermentation process, making it more stable.

The final point to consider is that fermentation will produce an element of alcohol. While it might only be a very small amount, it is still there. So best not to serve your ferments to anyone wanting to avoid alcohol altogether.

Fine strainer

While a small, fine strainer looks elegant, a larger one – that would normally be used for sifting flour – will work too. Just strain off the ice first, then pour your drink out slowly through the middle of the strainer. Removing the ice first will allow you to pour through the large strainer more accurately, without spilling down the side of the glass.

Ice

Most of the recipes in this book call for ice, so fill up your ice-cube tray well in advance of mixing your drinks. Most recipes use ice cubes, but some use crushed or rock ice. Behind the bar, we have different kinds of ice delivered, but you can recreate the same shapes and textures at home. For crushed ice, simply gather up some ice cubes in a clean tea towel (dish towel) and use a hammer or pestle to pound the ice to chips. For rock ice, fill an empty plastic container with filtered water, cover and freeze until frozen solid. To cut pieces of rock ice, carefully turn out the large cube onto a chopping board covered with a tea towel. Using another tea towel to grip the ice cube – and, crucially, protecting your hand – cut slabs of ice off the cube with a large, serrated knife. You can then cut smaller blocks from the slabs. The benefit of using rock ice is that it melts slowly and won't dilute the drink like ice cubes do.

Juicing

For those who do not have access to a centrifugal juicer (that's most of us), the best way to extract juice is to use a blender or a food processor. Start by peeling the fruit or vegetables, if needed, then segmenting them before blitzing in a blender or food processor. Once blitzed, pass the juice through a fine-mesh sieve lined with muslin (cheesecloth) into a sterilised glass bottle (see opposite). The muslin can be wound tight to squeeze out as much liquid as possible.

To extract fruit juice and pulp, you needn't own an immersion blender or food processor. Instead, place the fruit in a sturdy plastic container or metal tray and, using a potato masher or pestle, squash and muddle the fruit. After breaking it down as much as you can, transfer the fruit to a resealable bag, seal, and use a rolling pin to break it down even more. If the juice is required, pass the pulp through a fine-mesh sieve lined with muslin (cheesecloth).

Muddling stick

Muddling breaks up citrus, herbs or other solids when making a cocktail. In essence, this is just a fancy-shaped stick. A rolling pin will work just fine.

Oven dehydrating

Very few of us have access to restaurant dehydrators, but we can get the same results at home using the oven. Oven-drying is great for making citrus wheels, dried rounds of apple or poached rhubarb stems (just poach gently in a little water and sugar before drying).

Start by lining a baking tray with baking paper and preheating the oven to 60°C (140°F). Prepare a sugar syrup (see page 217) and add 2 per cent citric acid by weight (this will stop the sugar syrup from browning). Add the fruit to the syrup and stir gently to coat, then transfer the fruit to a baking tray and dry in the oven for eight hours. Make sure to turn the fruit after the first two hours to avoid it sticking.

If you do have access to a dehydrator, follow the same process using a tray in the dehydrator instead – set it to 60°C (140°F) and run it for the same amount of time. Store the dehydrated fruit in an airtight container in a cool, dry place and it will last for up to two months.

Peeler

We recommend getting your hands on a U-bend peeler as they are the easiest to drag down the side of a large orange. However, a regular vegetable peeler will suffice. Just make sure that you have a good grip and always pull away from yourself. If there are no peelers in the house, a regular knife (serrated works best) is good too: lay the peel down, pith side up, on a chopping board and scrape away any excess pith with the knife. Always cut and scrape away from yourself – safety first!

Shaker tin

Shaker tins are great, and the crack that you hear when separating the tins is the sound of success. However, any jar that has a good seal, such as a screw-top jar, will work. A jar can also be used as a serving vessel, which will save on some washing up. Win-win.

Sterilising bottles & jars

There are a number of ways to sterilise jars and containers. The first and easiest is to put them (including the lids) in a dishwasher and run it on a slow cycle. This will slowly bring the temperature up to a point where any bacteria is killed. Once the cycle is finished, place the jars on a clean tea towel (dish towel) to air-dry.

Alternatively, you can use an oven. This is the preferred method for sterilising jars for jams and jellies. Preheat the oven to 120°C (250°F). While it is heating, wash the jars and lids in hot, soapy water. Place the jars and lids on a baking tray and transfer to the oven for twenty minutes to fully dry out. Fill the jars immediately after removing from the oven and seal with the lids.

Storage

Storing fruits and vegetables

The fridge crisper is a great place to start. Most modern fridges are designed to regulate temperature and humidity, but a good tip is to not fill it right to the brim, as there needs to be adequate air flow around the produce. Also, it is important to make sure there is no fruit that is breaking down – it will spread mould and tarnish everything around it.

Fruits and vegetables should be separated in the fridge, as they will ripen at different rates.

Fruit that is bought under-ripe should be left on the kitchen bench for a couple of days to ripen naturally before being eaten. If you're in a hurry, put them in a fruit bowl with your bananas, as they release high levels of ethylene gas, which will naturally speed up the ripening of other fruits.

Storing dry goods

Make sure that spices and dried goods are stored in airtight containers in a dark, dry place. I usually layer dehydrated fruit and veg with paper towel so that any moisture is wicked away.

Storing syrups and other prep items

Syrup and other pre-prepared items should ideally be stored in the fridge. The lower temperature will give the prepped items more stability and a longer shelf life. Left out of the fridge, these products will break down and spoil.

Freezing

If you are unable to use your fresh fruit and vegetables straight away, they can be preserved in the freezer. Clean the fruits, then cut into segments and place in a reusable container (preferably one with a rubber seal). Leaving the peel on to freeze will help preserve the fruit.

With most vegetables, it is best to flash blanch them first. To do this, segment your vegetables, then blanch them in a saucepan of boiling water for thirty seconds. Remove and immediately plunge them into an ice bath, then freeze. This will trap both the colour and flavour so that when it comes time to use the produce, it is still as close to fresh as possible.

Freezing will lengthen the life of produce by two months.

Strainer (Hawthorne)

Probably the hardest piece of bar equipment to do without, but anything is possible. Whenever I leave my kit at an event or a friend's house, I look to the slotted spatula for this task. Just line it up while the tin or jar is upright, making sure that one of the slots lines up with the edge of the tin, then pour away. Alternatively, if you are proficient with chopsticks, use them to hold back the ice. Otherwise, two forks work just as well.

Straws

Understandably, plastic straws have been the first of many single-use plastic items to be targeted in the effort to reduce plastic waste. For those who want the straw minus the plastic, there are some fantastic options coming onto the market. Good-quality, thick paper straws are biodegradable and often come in fun designs. But if you entertain regularly, it's worth investing in metal straws. These make for a great drinking experience and are dishwasher-safe. New options such as straws made of bamboo or straw also work well, look great and are made from organic materials.

Tea bags

Home-made tea bags (for flavouring punches, individual teas, or even for making stocks and sauces) can be made from muslin (cheesecloth) or a clean cloth. Just lay a square of cloth out flat, place the herbs or spices in the centre, then draw the corners together in the middle. Tie off the bag with twine or an elastic band. Once used, compost the spices, hand-wash the cloth in warm water and air-dry, ready for the next use.

Vinegars

Instead of making a natural vinegar, which takes quite some time, you can always flavour an existing vinegar instead. Depending on what the end goal is, you can do this a couple of ways.

To make a vinegar as a flavouring element (similar to aromatic bitters), I like to use a neutral vinegar base, such as rice vinegar, and add a ratio of 10 per cent spice to vinegar. Combine the desired spice and vinegar in an airtight container, seal and leave to sit at room temperature for three days to one week, tasting every day until you're happy with the flavour. Strain, bottle and seal.

For a drinking vinegar, it is best to use a combination of vinegars and water. My preferred ratio is two parts apple-cider vinegar, one part white-wine vinegar and one part water. This will give a slightly milder mix, better for the larger volumes used in cocktails. To flavour your vinegar, simply add 10 per cent (by weight) of fruit or spice, or a combination of the two, and leave to sit at room temperature for three days in an airtight container. Strain, then bottle and seal it.

These vinegars are best stored in the fridge.

Zesting citrus before juicing

Always peel your citrus fruits before juicing them and reserve the peel for using in cordials or as a garnish. If you are making cocktails that require citrus twists, simply wrap the peels in wet paper and store them in the fridge for use that day. If you're not planning to use them on the same day, freeze the peels ready for your next batch of tonic syrup, or to flavour cordials or vinegars.

Citrus

The first thing to understand about citrus is that the citrus fruits we know today are actually hybrid varieties of four original ones: mandarin, pomelo, citron and papeda. And the citrus family is growing all the time as farmers crossbreed their citrus to produce more unique offerings of desirable fruit.

The second thing is that a lot of citrus fruits come into season in winter, which comes as a surprise to a lot of people. We associate that fresh, juicy, zingy kick of citrus with good times in the hot weather, but often that citrus you're enjoying has travelled a long way to arrive in your summer cocktail. You see, we are spoilt for choice; if we want a blood orange in the middle of summer, then someone will import it for us from the opposite hemisphere. One of our reasons for writing this book was to help remind people that seasonal and local is best, and that we don't *need* to have certain fruits and veg at certain times of the year. Citrus is a prime example of this, especially if we look at lemons and limes, which are probably the two most heavily used varieties in bars. A lot of bars will carry them throughout the year, regardless of the season, to make sure customers can have their G&T with lemon or their margarita with lime, mainly because bars are there to meet the demands of the customer. We need to change that way of thinking. There is citrus fruit available in different varieties all year round and, I'll give you a hot tip, they are all delicious in a G&T!

One last note on citrus fruit before we get stuck in to the recipes: fresh is best. Once citrus is juiced, you should ideally use it within a few hours. If you leave it any longer, you will notice a deterioration in flavour and some funky, metallic notes coming through.

Sweet orange

These are the types of oranges I grew up with. They were packed in my lunchbox for a snack and served at half-time in football matches. Fast forward to today and I still enjoy an orange or three, albeit in juicy liquid form with a splash of gin.

There are three main varieties of sweet orange: navel, valencia and blood. Valencias are famed for their juice and make the perfect addition to that summer mimosa, whereas navels are favoured for their flesh. Blood oranges sit in both camps for me: I love blood orange juice and I love using blood orange segments in salads.

BLOOD

NAVEL

VALENCIA

SPRING   SUMMER   AUTUMN   WINTER

Orange sherbet 💧

MAKES APPROX. 750 ML (25½ FL OZ)

5 sweet oranges of your
    choice
caster (superfine) sugar

To make a sherbet, we must first learn a little Latin. The process involves preparing an *oleo saccharum*, which translates as sugar oil. When you combine caster sugar with fresh citrus peel, the sugar draws out the citrus oils, making a really fragrant sugar oil. When this sugar oil is combined with the juice from that same citrus fruit, we have what's called a sherbet. This process can be used for any citrus fruit and is a great way to showcase the whole flavour of the fruit, including the zest, in liquid form.

Peel the oranges with a vegetable peeler. Juice them and measure out the total quantity of juice. In a separate bowl, measure out the same quantity of sugar. Refrigerate the juice until needed.

Combine the peels and sugar in a bowl and leave to rest in a warm place for 2 hours, stirring every 30 minutes. Add the juice to the sugar mixture and stir to dissolve.

Strain into a sterilised glass bottle and seal. Refrigerate for up to 1 week.

For another day

Just add soda. As simple as it seems, just start with 50:50 soda and sherbet over ice and continue adding more soda until you hit that sweet spot.

Spike my G&T. That's right, bring a little orange to your G&T – but just a splash, as you still want to taste that gin.

Salad dressing. Cut the sherbet with white-wine vinegar and olive oil for a delightful salad dressing. Start with an equal-parts blend and adjust to taste.

Gayndah fizz ⬦

60 ml (2 fl oz) Orange
  sherbet (opposite)
1 egg yolk
1 teaspoon honey
  (preferably a lighter one,
  such as orange blossom)
ice cubes, for shaking
60 ml (2 fl oz) soda water
  (club soda)
freshly grated nutmeg,
  to garnish

The name of this cocktail may seem a little strange, so let me explain the journey. A *golden* fizz uses the yolk of an egg, a *silver* fizz the white, and a royale uses the whole thing. Looking at the ingredients for this cocktail, what we had was a golden orange fizz. However, a quick internet search revealed a pub in Queensland called the Golden Orange, located in Gayndah. The icing on the cake was reading about Gayndah and finding out they have an orange festival that has been running for sixty years! Cocktail name sorted.

Shake the sherbet, egg yolk and honey with ice cubes, then strain into a highball glass.

Gently top with soda water and more ice. Garnish with freshly grated nutmeg.

Cobbler on a rock

60 ml (2 fl oz) sherry
  (see *Notes*)
15 ml (½ fl oz) Orange
  sherbet (opposite)
dash of absinthe
  (see *Notes*)
ice cubes, for shaking
piece of rock ice, to serve
fresh, whole, seasonal
  berries, to garnish
  (raspberries are my pick)

Cobblers have been around for quite some time. Essentially, it's a simple combination of citrus, sherry and sugar served over crushed ice. I heard once that in the 1800s crushed ice was considered a status symbol, as ice was such an expensive commodity, and ordering your cobbler over crushed ice was a way of showing off your wealth. I'm not sure how true that is, but I do know that I'm not a fan of crushed ice for this particular cocktail as it dilutes too quickly. I suggest serving it over a large rock of ice, which will melt slowly and keep the drink nice and cool.

Shake all the ingredients with ice cubes, then strain over a large piece of rock ice into an old fashioned glass.

Garnish with seasonal berries.

A local, sherry-like product (such as Amontillado) works well here.

A local, anise-flavoured spirit would work just as well in place of absinthe.

Mandarin

This was very much a lunchbox special when I was a kid, so much so that it put me off them for years. A mandarin forgotten in the bottom of a school bag for weeks on end wasn't pleasant.

There are many varieties of mandarin, but to me the two most important are the imperial (which appears at the start of the season and contains a few pips) and the murcott (which comes at the end of the season and contains lots of pips). Imperials are easier to peel, but the juice of the murcott is oh so sweet and perfect for juicing.

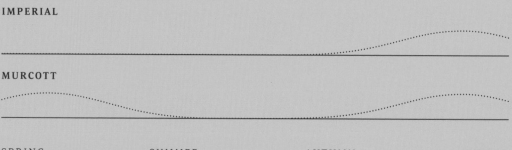

IMPERIAL

MURCOTT

SPRING   SUMMER   AUTUMN   WINTER

Mandarin shrub ◌

**MAKES APPROX. 500 ML
(17 FL OZ/2 CUPS)**

2 mandarins
caster (superfine) sugar
light sherry vinegar

Nick and I developed this recipe during our time at Gin Palace for the winter cocktail list of 2013. The cocktail we created with it was a boozy one that also contained gin, pear cider and a touch of mezcal – not something destined for the pages of a low- and no-alcohol cocktail bible. But the drink was great, and I believe it was due to the combination of the smoke from the mezcal and the oxidative characteristics of the sherry vinegar. Bacon and mandarin salad, anyone?

Peel the mandarins, setting aside the peel, and weigh the flesh. Place the mandarin flesh in a bowl and add the same weight of sugar to it. For every gram of mandarin flesh, add 1 ml of sherry vinegar, then blitz it all with a stick blender.

Strain and pour the shrub into a sterilised glass jar (see page 15) with the mandarin skins and refrigerate for up to 1 week.

For another day

Just add soda. Start with 50:50 shrub and soda water (club soda) over ice and add more soda to taste.

Chicken salad dressing. Well, any salad would work, but I just love chicken salad with walnuts and a 50:50 ratio of shrub to olive oil for the dressing.

Pickled dates. Soak some pitted dates in the shrub for 1 week, then remove and serve them draped with pickled ginger. You'll be in for quite the ride.

Minted reticulata

Minted reticulata

30 ml (1 fl oz) Mandarin
  shrub (page 25)
30 ml (1 fl oz) dry sherry
  (see *Note*)
60 ml (2 fl oz) Minted
  water (see below)
ice cubes, to serve
thyme sprig, to garnish

MINTED WATER
fresh mint leaves

The Mandarin shrub is made with sherry vinegar, so we know sherry is going to work well here and, for those of you not in the know, the alluring waft of thyme over the top of a mandarin cocktail is something special. This is a perfect pre-dinner cocktail, as it's light, juicy and will get those tastebuds going. The minted water also has other uses. I love it during summer, as it takes the edge off plain water and is incredibly refreshing. The only issue with it is that it doesn't last long – a couple of days at the most – so if you make some, drink it up!

For the minted water, combine the mint leaves with water – about 20 g (¾ oz) leaves for every 1 litre (34 fl oz/4 cups) should do it – in a bowl and leave to macerate for 1 hour. Strain the water through a fine-mesh sieve and refrigerate. Must be used on the same day it is made.

Combine all the ingredients in a highball glass and top with ice cubes. Gently stir. Garnish with thyme and imbibe.

Local sherry-type products are always preferred. Save the sherry for that holiday in Jerez.

Smoked reticulata

100 ml (3½ fl oz) ginger
  beer
40 ml (1¼ fl oz) Mandarin
  shrub (page 25)
2 dashes of hot sauce
2 drops of liquid smoke
ice cubes, to serve
pistachio nuts, to serve

In case you're wondering, reticulata is the species of citrus that mandarins belong to. I like to think that I am good at creating cocktails, but naming them has never been my strong suit. As I mentioned earlier, I find that smoke and mandarin work really well together, so I decided to mix the shrub with some liquid smoke, which is, as you can guess, smoke in liquid form. You can pick it up at barbecue supply stores and add it to your meat or dips, or just your cocktails!

Combine all the ingredients in a highball glass and top with ice. Gently stir. Serve with pistachios to enjoy on the side.

Lemon

As they say, when life gives you lemons ... order a G&T. Actually, it's not just the G&T, but a multitude of classic cocktails that call for lemon juice, and we all know (or should know) that fresh juice is the best juice. Because of this, a lot of bars carry lemons throughout the year, even if it means importing them from far away. This isn't a sustainable approach, so, when working with lemons, consider the season and how far they have travelled to get into your glass.

There are quite a number of varieties, but the ones I am most familiar with are Meyer lemons (the sweeter ones) and eureka (the tarter ones). One variety that I am not too familiar with in its raw form is the Sorrento, which can be most commonly found on the Amalfi Coast in Italy, although not exclusively. I heard once that more than fifty per cent of Sorrento lemons in Italy go into limoncello. I'm not sure if that's strictly true, but it certainly showcases how best to use them.

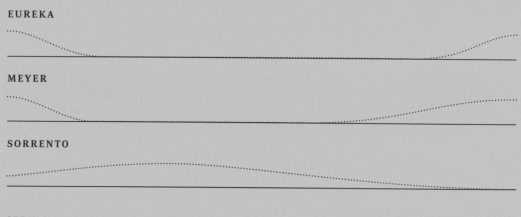

EUREKA

MEYER

SORRENTO

SPRING　　　　　SUMMER　　　　　AUTUMN　　　　　WINTER

Limoncello

**MAKES APPROX.
1.5 LITRES (51 FL OZ/
6 CUPS)**

2 kg (4 lb 6 oz) lemons
250 g (9 oz) caster
  (superfine) sugar
700 ml (23½ fl oz) vodka
250 ml (8½ fl oz/1 cup)
  white port
10 g (¼ oz) dried lemon
  balm

If you aren't on the Amalfi Coast and don't have access to Sorrento lemons, fear not; any lemons will work for this recipe. It is a two-step process, which can be viewed as the 'sweet lemon vodka thingy' and the 'porty lemony stuff'. The port doesn't have to be from Portugal (something local that represents its style is fine), but it does have to be white as tannins don't play well here. Charring the lemons gives them a smoky intensity and an extra layer of complexity. For me, limoncello can taste quite plain, but a few extra elements can make it wonderful. One last note: once you have finished making the 'sweet lemon vodka thingy', take the lemons, slice them into wheels and dehydrate them (see page 15), as they make a great garnish. You will need to start this recipe about one month ahead of time.

Peel the lemons and combine the peel and sugar in a sealable 1 litre (34 fl oz/4 cup) jar. Leave to rest for 2 weeks in the fridge.

Halve the lemons crossways and char, flesh-side down, in a dry griddle pan set over a high heat for about 1 minute.

Combine the charred lemons with the vodka in an airtight container and leave to rest for 2 weeks at room temperature.

Mix the white port and lemon balm together in a sealable jar and leave to rest for 1 day.

Add 700 ml (23½ fl oz) water to the lemon peel and sugar and stir to dissolve. Strain the vodka, white port, and water and sugar mixtures through a coffee filter or a piece of muslin (cheesecloth) into a large bowl or saucepan. Stir until well combined, then pour into sterilised glass bottles. The limoncello will keep for up to 1 year in the fridge.

For another day

Ice cream. Drizzle some over your dessert.

Chicken marinade. Coat some chicken in limoncello and marinate overnight before chargrilling it.

Earl Grey tea. Spike your tea with just a splash of limoncello.

Limoncello collins

60 ml (2 fl oz) soda water
  (club soda)
45 ml (1½ fl oz) hydrosol
30 ml (1 fl oz) Limoncello
  (page 29)
ice cubes, to serve
dehydrated charred lemon
  (see page 14), to garnish

The most famous Collins is a Tom, of course. A simple mix of gin, lemon, sugar and the bubbliest of water was prescribed to quench the thirst and enliven the party. In this version, the limoncello ticks two of those boxes – just add soda water (club soda). In the past few years, we have seen hydrosols hit the market, which are, essentially, distillates without the booze. Seedlip is probably the most well known and widely available brand, and they have a few boozless alternatives to gin. Their Spice 94 works really well here, but I have also used other hydrosols to much success, so the moral of the story is (as always): try to find something local first but if you can't, then this is a good option.

Gently combine all the ingredients in a highball or collins glass, then carefully top with ice cubes to retain the fizz.

Garnish with dehydrated lemon.

Tartening of the fennel

45 ml (1½ fl oz) Limoncello
  (page 29)
45 ml (1½ fl oz) fennel
  juice (see intro)
dash of Orange bitters
  (page 42)
dash of absinthe
ice cubes, for shaking
dehydrated charred lemon
  (see page 14), to garnish
1 fennel frond, to garnish

The older I get, the more I love fennel. It just has so much to offer: the pollen, the fronds, the bulbs, the seeds, each with delightful, subtle differences in aroma and flavour. For this cocktail, we take the bulb, which is wonderfully fresh, and juice it to make fennel juice. The best way to accomplish this is to use a centrifugal juicer, but if you don't have access to one then simply blitz the bulb to a purée and squeeze the liquid through a clean tea towel (dish towel).

Shake all the ingredients with the ice cubes and strain into a cocktail glass.

Garnish with dehydrated lemon and a fennel frond.

Lime

Mai tais and mojitos and margaritas, oh my! The refreshing acidic kick of lime is the reason they are a staple in many cocktails and, of course, behind the bar. However, not all limes were created equal. There is quite the range, and they all have different uses. Finger limes, for example, have caviar-like pearls that burst in your mouth and are delightful served on top of oysters. Kaffir lime, on the other hand, is prized for its leaves rather than its fruit. Each year I visit a friend who has a tree to grab some leaves for the annual production of Maidenii vermouth, and each year I grab a couple of limes as well to try to do something interesting with them. Tahitian, or Persian, and key limes are other important varieties, and these are the ones best suited to use in drinks.

FINGER

KAFFIR

KEY

TAHITIAN

SPRING   SUMMER   AUTUMN   WINTER

Lime cordial ⬡

MAKES APPROX. 500 ML (17 FL OZ/2 CUPS)

30 g (1 oz) lime zest (from approx. 10 limes)
350 g (12½ oz) caster (superfine) sugar
10 g (¼ oz) citric acid

This was one of the first bar prep recipes I developed when I started at Gin Palace. The idea came about after I saw how many limes we threw out after juicing them – lime zest is too good to waste, after all. So we would zest the limes at the start of the weekend, then use the fruit to juice over the course of the weekend, essentially using up the whole fruit. If you're not planning a lime juice fiesta, you can also slice the limes after microplaning them, soak them in maple syrup and dehydrate them (see page 14) to use as garnishes. You will need to start this cordial recipe five days ahead of time.

Zest the limes with a microplane and set aside.

Combine the sugar and citric acid with 350 ml (12 fl oz) water in a saucepan. Heat gently over a low heat to dissolve the sugar, then remove from the heat and pour into a sterilised jar (see page 15). Add the lime zest, then refrigerate for 5 days.

Pass the cordial through a fine-mesh sieve and pour into a sterilised bottle (see page 15). Store in the fridge for up to 1 month.

For another day

Coconut water. Sometimes coconut water can feel a bit heavy in the mouth; this cordial, or even a squeeze of fresh lime, does wonders to liven it up.

Wheat beer. Just a dash of this cordial pumps up the summer vibe to an eleven out of ten.

Gimlet. The classic lime cordial cocktail, but probably not one for these pages as it does contain a hefty amount of booze. However, if you must, shake two parts gin with one part lime cordial and ice, then strain into a cocktail glass.

Molasses & lime

45 ml (1½ fl oz) verjus (see
 page 218)
30 ml (1 fl oz) Lime cordial
 (opposite)
1 teaspoon molasses
ice cubes, for shaking
dehydrated lime wheel
 (see page 14), to garnish

The inspiration for this drink is the classic daiquiri combination
of rum, lime and sugar. Our cordial provides two of those parts and
the molasses steps in for the rum (rum being made from molasses).
A word of warning: a little bit of molasses goes a long way and
it is not the prettiest substance, which means that, unfortunately,
this cocktail isn't the most photogenic. But it sure is refreshing.

Shake all the ingredients with ice cubes, then strain into a cocktail
glass.

Garnish with dehydrated lime and enjoy.

The polariser

small handful of coriander
 (cilantro) leaves
15 ml (½ fl oz) anise liqueur
 (see *Note*)
30 ml (1 fl oz) fresh lime
 juice
90 ml (3 fl oz) dry ginger ale
ice cubes, to serve
kaffir lime leaf, to garnish

Anise and coriander (cilantro) are two ingredients that really
polarise people, hence the name. They are also two ingredients
that work well together. Lime really brings it all together, giving
a refreshing and balancing break from the intensity of the
ingredients.

Add the coriander to a highball glass and muddle very gently.
Add the anise and lime juice, and gently top up with ginger ale.

Carefully finish with ice and garnish with a kaffir lime leaf.

*Pastis is a good option here, as is absinthe, but try to find
something local if you can.*

Grapefruit

It wasn't until I was a little older that I started enjoying grapefruit, which I assume was due to the slight bitterness of the fruit. You see, bitterness is something you have to train your body to like because we, as humans, are hardwired to perceive bitterness as poison. The brain tells the palate 'no, no, no'. Luckily, I have educated my palate over the years to love this slightly bitter citrus. There are a number of varieties and crossbreeds, but the two main varieties are white and red grapefruits. The white ones are a little more tart and bitter, whereas the red ones are on the sweeter side.

RUBY RED

WHITE

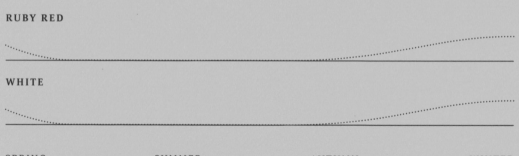

SPRING   SUMMER   AUTUMN   WINTER

Grapefruit granita

**MAKES APPROX. 500 G
(1 LB 2 OZ)**

250 g (9 oz) caster
  (superfine) sugar
5 grapefruits
150 ml (5 fl oz) quinquina
1 egg white

A granita can be as simple as freezing fruit juice and scraping the solid mass every half an hour or so. The scraping helps to aerate the frozen juice, making it lighter to eat. In this recipe, we've added some egg white to help with this process. We also use a cream charger to get as much air into the granita as possible (we've included instructions on how to make this without one, but it will take a little longer). It is important to note that, depending on the sweetness of the grapefruit, you may need to adjust the quantity of sugar, adding more juice or more sugar to taste. Once you have added the quinquina but before adding the egg, taste the liquid and adjust, but bear in mind that the sweetness will drop off a little once the granita has frozen. You will need to start this recipe at least three hours ahead of time (seven hours if you're not using a cream charger).

Start by dissolving the sugar in 250 ml (8 fl oz/1 cup) water in a saucepan over a low heat. Once dissolved, remove from the heat and leave to cool.

Zest and juice the grapefruits.

If you have a 1 litre (34 fl oz/4 cup) cream charger, put the zest and juice into the canister. Add the quinquina, then double charge the canister and shake for 5 minutes before expressing the gas. Strain the contents through a fine-mesh sieve, discarding the grapefruit zest, and return the liquid to the canister with the sugar syrup and egg white. Double charge the canister again, shake for 2 minutes, then discharge onto a baking tray.

If you don't have a cream charger, combine the zest in a bowl with the grapefruit juice and quinquina, and leave to soak in the fridge for 4 hours. Strain through a fine-mesh sieve, discarding the grapefruit zest, then combine with the sugar syrup and egg white. Whisk for 2 minutes and transfer the mixture onto a baking tray.

Transfer the tray to the freezer and leave for 3 hours. Every 30 minutes, remove the granita from the freezer and scrape it with a fork to aerate so that it doesn't freeze in chunks. Covered, the granita will last for 2 months in the freezer.

For another day

Palate cleanser. The tart, refreshing nature of granita makes it an ideal palate cleanser between courses at dinner.

Pair it with goat's cheese. The flavours really work well together.

Grapefruit spritz. Just top with soda – it doesn't even need ice!

Grapefruit granita

Sake snow cone

Sake snow cone

30 ml (1 fl oz) sake
  (see *Note*)
15 ml (½ fl oz) sparkling
  wine
4 drops of Saline solution
  (page 216)
2 tablespoons Grapefruit
  granita (page 37)
rosemary sprig, to garnish

Sake doesn't have to be one of those things that you only have when visiting a Japanese restaurant. It actually makes for a great cocktail as it offers something that is not commonly found in any other liquor: umami. This rich 'meatiness' can vary between different varieties, but it's great paired with grapefruit and salt, as it contrasts well with the flavour of the sake. Believe it or not, sake is produced in countries other than Japan. It might take a bit more digging, but they are out there, so see if you can find a local one.

Combine the sake, wine and saline solution in a small glass. Top with the granita and garnish with the rosemary sprig.

Serve with a spoon and a straw (not a plastic one!).

Something dry, light and local is best here.

The forbidden cocktail

6 fresh sage leaves
100 ml (3½ fl oz) soda
  water (club soda)
3 tablespoons Grapefruit
  granita (page 37)
freshly grated nutmeg,
  to garnish

When grapefruits (originally a cross between a sweet orange and a pomelo) were discovered, they were known as the forbidden fruit. Grapefruit juice is known to interact with some medications, making them over or underactive. Sage, another ingredient in this cocktail, contains thujone, a GABA antagonist that, in significant amounts, slows cognition and focus. Plus, the nutmeg garnish contains a psychoactive drug called myristicin. All in all, a pretty foreboding drink. The soda water, however, is fine, unless you don't like bubbles ...

Put the sage leaves in a highball glass and muddle very gently. Carefully pour in the soda, then add the granita.

Stir gently to combine, then garnish with the nutmeg.

Bitter orange

Whereas sweet oranges are more prized in the food industry, bitter oranges are more prized by the liquor industry. From witbier in Belgium, to chinato in Italy and various liqueurs in France, bitter oranges are sought out for their zest, which is so incredibly aromatic and, funnily enough, bitter.

A couple of well-known examples of bitter orange are bergamot (used to make Earl Grey tea) and chinotto (used to make the Italian soda of the same name). Bitter oranges are also used to make neroli oil, which has uses in both the homeopathic industry and the soft-drink industry (some even claim that it is used to make Coca-Cola!).

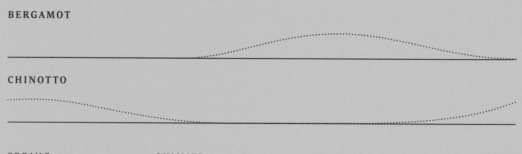

BERGAMOT

CHINOTTO

SPRING   SUMMER   AUTUMN   WINTER

Orange bitters

**MAKES 500 ML
(17 FL OZ/2 CUPS)**

SPICED ORANGE SOAK
200 ml (7 fl oz) 95 per cent
  spirit (see *Note*)
100 g (3½ oz) bitter
  orange zest
10 g (¼ oz) cacao nibs
10 g (¼ oz) coriander
  seeds
5 g (⅛ oz) angelica root
1 cinnamon stick

BITTERED WATER
100 g (3½ oz) brown sugar
5 g (⅛ oz) gentian root

Cocktail bitters are incredibly useful to have lying around, not only for mixed drinks, but also for food. I always seem to be grabbing for a bottle of bitters when I'm making a stew or pasta sauce to give it an extra kick of flavour without adding too much liquid. That's the great thing about bitters: a little goes a long way. You will notice this recipe is broken up into two parts – the spiced orange soak and the bittered water. This is because bitterness is more soluble in water than it is in ethanol, and this gives us a more bitter result. Don't forget to juice the oranges after peeling them (see page 13); bitter orange juice mixed with vermouth and soda makes for quite the delightful spritz. You'll need to start this recipe one month ahead of time.

For the spiced orange soak, combine all the ingredients in a sealable jar with 50 ml (1¾ fl oz) water. Leave it somewhere visible so it doesn't slip your mind, and shake it once a day for a month. Strain through a coffee filter, paper towel or clean, disposable cloth and store in the fridge.

Once the soak is ready, prepare the bittered water. Combine the gentian root and sugar in a saucepan with 500 ml (17 fl oz/2 cups) water and heat gently. Simmer until the liquid has reduced by half, then strain through a coffee filter, paper towel or clean, disposable cloth. Mix with the strained orange soak and pour into a sterilised glass bottle (see page 15). Sealed, the soak will keep for at least 1 year in the fridge.

You can buy 95 per cent spirit (also known as rectified spirit) from your friendly local distiller or online.

For another day

Orange hot chocolate. Chocolate and orange have been mates for a long time – even longer than peas and carrots! Add a dash to your favourite hot chocolate for an extra orange kick.

Hummus. My wife loves hummus, so we always have some in the fridge. I'm not as excited by the chickpea dip as she is, until I add a splash of bitters.

Seville spritz

45 ml (1½ fl oz)
  medium–dry vermouth
  (see *Note*)
45 ml (1½ fl oz) bitter
  orange juice
45 ml (1½ fl oz) soda water
  (club soda)
ice cubes, to serve
basil leaf, to garnish

Bitter oranges are also known as Seville oranges, hence the name of this spritz. This drink makes so much sense. Spritzes are meant to be light, bitter and bubbly, and the juice of the bitter orange brings the bitterness while balancing out the sweetness of the vermouth. The soda lifts it all up to be light and refreshing, but the only problem with this drink is that bitter oranges are a winter fruit, meaning we can't enjoy them in the warm sunshine. The solution? Crank the heating up and put your feet in a bucket of sand while enjoying this bitter spritz.

Gently combine the ingredients in a wine glass, then carefully top with ice cubes to retain the fizz.

Garnish with a basil leaf.

Bianco-style vermouths work quite well, as do quinquinas.

Tea toddy

5 g (⅛ oz) lapsang
  souchong tea
20 g (¾ oz) malted barley
150 ml (5 fl oz) boiling
  water
1 teaspoon
  strong-flavoured honey,
  such as leatherwood
  or manuka
3 dashes of Orange bitters
  (opposite)

As soon as I get a cold, I reach for this recipe. Depending on how bad the cold is, I sometimes even add a splash of brandy too. Lapsang souchong tea is a smoked black tea that has great body and weight, making it quite suitable for mixing with strong flavours. Because of this, you can pair it with strong-flavoured honeys. I lean towards leatherwood, which is quite an intense honey with hints of menthol – delightful in this tea toddy.

Mix the tea, barley and water in a bowl or jug and leave to infuse for 2 minutes. Strain into a teacup and add the honey and bitters. Stir to dissolve, then drink.

Berries

Berries played such a key role in my food memories growing up, from making up sweet treats, to friends (in Brisbane, Queensland) bringing them to school during end-of-year exams (early summer). When I started university, I got a job at the local fruit and vegetable shop, Milton Fruit Bowl, which led to summers of making sure punnets of berries were at their peak, free from breakdown, and creating an appealing display of produce to draw in customers. Berries, including grapes, made up the summer's most alluring displays.

Following my studies, I moved into the bar world, and berries were always abundant during the festive season. This allowed us to fanicify our cocktail garnishes easily and get through the queues quickly, which were usually four deep at the bar.

What technically defines a berry is their embedded seeds, which, interestingly, means that strawberries, raspberries and blackberries are not really berries – confusing, considering their names.

–Nick

Strawberry

Strawberries are the showpiece of the berry season and, at the same time, the greatest example of how much better fruit is in the peak of its natural season. In the height of summer, strawberries are sweet and acidic, evoking early childhood memories of gummy worms. Out-of-season strawberries, which can be bought year-round, are often bland and chalky.

At the royal shows and country fairs in Australia, the highlight is always the charity stalls selling strawberry ice cream with fresh strawberries. And as an adult, they're just about the only reason for braving the crowds.

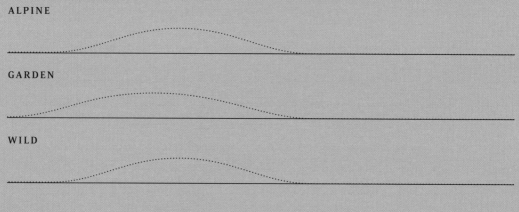

ALPINE

GARDEN

WILD

SPRING   SUMMER   AUTUMN   WINTER

Strawberry-top kefir

**MAKES 1.5 LITRES
(51 FL OZ/6 CUPS)**

75 g (2¾ oz) cane sugar
1.5 litres (51 fl oz/6 cups)
  boiling water
strawberry tops from
  250 g (9 oz) strawberries
  (approx. 1 punnet)
3 tablespoons water kefir
  grains
1 lemon, halved
100 ml (3½ fl oz) apple
  juice (see *Note*)

Kefir is a fermentation using a SCOBY (symbiotic culture of bacteria and yeast). In this case, a water-grain kefir breaks down the sugars in the solution, converting it into a dry, sour, slightly alcoholic (less than 1 per cent alcohol by volume, or ABV) beverage. You can buy these grains from good health-food stores. This recipe is courtesy of Vicky Simmington, one of the founders of the Grow symposium. Because the fermentation takes time, you'll need to start this recipe about one week before you want to drink it.

Combine the sugar and boiling water, and stir until the sugar has dissolved. Set aside to cool. Once cool, add the strawberry tops, kefir grains and lemon halves. Transfer to a sterilised glass jar, cover with a piece of muslin (cheesecloth) and leave it to sit for 2–3 days, tasting as you go to achieve your desired sourness.

Strain the liquid through a fine-mesh sieve and pour into a sterilised glass bottle (see page 15) with the apple juice, then seal. This will give it a second fermentation and produce mild carbonation. After a couple more days, refrigerate the kefir, as this will stop the fermentation process. Stored in the fridge, it will keep for up to 1 month.

Store-bought apple juice is best, as it has been pasteurised.

For another day

Drink the kefir by itself. It's a delicious alternative to kombucha.

Enjoy it for breakfast. Add some strawberry kefir to your breakfast smoothie.

Fancify your G&T. Try half tonic, half kefir for a drier, delicious G&T.

Strawberry purée ice cubes

MAKES 6 ICE CUBES

250 g (9 oz) strawberries,
   hulled (approx. 1 punnet;
   use the strawberries
   from your Strawberry-
   top kefir, page 47)
50 g (1¾ oz) caster
   (superfine) sugar

These ice cubes remind me of my early school years. We would add them to glasses of cold water when we got home from school. As I got into bartending, I discovered that they made a fantastic addition to classic shaken cocktails. They can be added, along with ice cubes, when shaking drinks, turning the cocktail a brilliant blush pink, or they can be added to a built drink, such as a mojito, for a pop of colour and flavour.

Purée the strawberries and sugar using a food processor or a hand-held blender. Strain the mixture through a fine-mesh sieve to remove the seeds, then freeze the purée in a silicone ice-cube mould. The cubes will last up to 1 month in the freezer.

For another day

Rosé. Add strawberry purée cubes to your glass of rosé.

Dessert. Finely shave these ice cubes over a chocolatey dessert for a zip of flavour.

Salad dressing. Blitz them in a salad dressing for a fruity kick.

Sour strawberry spritz

60 ml (2 fl oz) Strawberry-
top kefir (page 47)
20 ml (¾ fl oz) aromatic
bitters
dash of orange-blossom
water
30 ml (1 fl oz) sparkling
wine
ice cubes, to serve
1 Strawberry purée ice
cube (page 48)
30 ml (1 fl oz) soda water
(club soda)
fresh strawberry, halved,
to garnish

The spritz has enjoyed something of renaissance in recent years, and for good reason – it is a fun and invigorating pre-dinner drink. I'm a big fan of sourness in my cocktails – not necessarily a classic citrus sour, but more the lactobacillus sour that we are seeing in sour beers. This recipe brings the level of sweetness down a notch and adds a sour touch with the Strawberry-top kefir.

Combine the kefir, bitters, orange-blossom water and sparkling wine in a wine glass and stir once. Add some ice cubes and the strawberry purée ice cube, then top with soda and garnish with the strawberry halves.

Temperance strawberry daiquiri

60 ml (2 fl oz) Strawberry-
top kefir (page 47)
20 ml (¾ fl oz) Lime cordial
(page 34)
10 ml (¼ fl oz) Brown sugar
syrup (page 217)
2 Strawberry purée ice
cubes (page 48)
2 grinds of fresh black
pepper
ice cubes, for shaking

Taking inspiration from more traditional strawberry daiquiri variations, this cocktail uses Strawberry-top kefir and Lime cordial to bring the sourness and acidity of the classic version. This is a refreshing and crowd-pleasing addition to any summer frivolity. Hot tip: whiz it in a blender with ice for a frozen daiquiri or frappé.

Combine all the ingredients with ice cubes and shake nice and hard so it gets super cold. Strain into a cocktail glass and become the star of the party!

Raspberry

Raspberries caused us the most grief at the fruit and veg store. They were the first fruit kids went for, pulling and squashing them everywhere, and the fragile berries didn't hold up very well. A daily chore was going through the punnets making sure none had whiskers (furry growth).

Though you might be most familiar with the common red, raspberries actually come in a variety of colours. Golden raspberries are beautifully sweet and light, while the black variety are slightly more savoury Of course, the star of the show is the traditional red: bright, juicy, acidic and heady. A self-contained sweet treat.

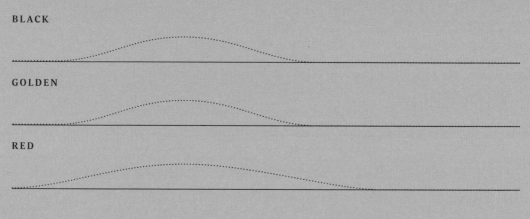

BLACK

GOLDEN

RED

SPRING   SUMMER   AUTUMN   WINTER

Raspberry cordial ⬨

**MAKES 500 ML
(17 FL OZ/2 CUPS)**

700 g (1 lb 9 oz)
  raspberries, frozen
350 g (12½ oz) fructose
  (see *Notes*)
7.5 g (⅛ oz) tartaric acid

This is a favourite recipe of ours – one that Shaun has been making for countless years. It is fantastic as it has the perfect amount of sweetness and acidity to balance out drinks, not to mention the bold red colour, which is enough to make any cocktail stand out. You will need to start this recipe one day in advance.

It's important to freeze your raspberries for this recipe, as this allows the fruit to break down better in the sugar.

Put the raspberries in a bowl with 70 g (2½ oz) of the fructose and refrigerate for 24 hours.

Carefully strain the raspberries (see *Notes*), reserving the liquid and making sure not to include any of the pulp. If you have the time, place the fruit in a piece of muslin (cheesecloth) and suspend it over a bowl to strain gradually. Add the remaining fructose and acid to the strained liquid, then mix with a hand-held blender until the fructose has dissolved.

Pour the cordial into a sterilised glass bottle (see page 15) and store for up to 1 week in the fridge.

You can find fructose at your local baking supplies shop.

Enjoy any leftover raspberry on top of natural yoghurt for breakfast.

For another day

Just add soda. Who doesn't love a good pink lemonade?

Make it creamy. Add to some whipped cream for a fluffy, rippled treat.

Great in a flora dora. With gin and ginger beer, even if it is a bit boozy.

Flip it! I like a little bit of cordial in my buttermilk pancake mix for a raspberry kick.

Naked batida

Naked batida ⬨

30 ml (1 fl oz) Raspberry
  cordial (page 51)
4 tablespoons natural
  yoghurt
10 ml (¼ fl oz) Vanilla syrup
  (page 217)
crushed ice, to serve
mint sprig, to garnish

This cocktail takes inspiration from a Brazilian cocktail called the batida, classically made with Cachaça. Batida roughly translates to 'milkshake' in Portuguese.

Combine all the ingredients and shake vigorously. Pour into a rocks glass over crushed ice.

Garnish with a mint sprig.

RTV

45 ml (1½ fl oz) verjus
  (see page 218)
20 ml (¾ fl oz) Raspberry
  cordial (page 51)
20 ml (¾ fl oz) Tonic syrup
  (page 219)
20 ml (¾ fl oz) white rum
ice cubes, for shaking
rosemary sprig, to garnish

For this recipe, I like to use a white rum; one with a virgin (unaged) cane base is preferable to one with a molasses base (though I know it's not technically a rum in Australia). Cane spirits have an incredible vegetal backbone that carries through drinks even when used in small amounts. These spirits are produced throughout the world, primarily in tropical regions where sugar cane is grown. Combined here with the acidity of the verjus (I like to use a local semillon grape one), the bitterness of the tonic and the brightness of the raspberry, it makes a fantastic aperitivo.

Combine all the ingredients in a shaker and shake vigorously, then strain into a cocktail glass.

Garnish with a rosemary sprig. If you're feeling fancy, give it a quick torch for a smoky aroma. You can do this on the barbecue, with a blowtorch or on a gas stove; just light the flame and then blow it quickly. Make sure you are safe and use tongs to hold the rosemary.

Blueberry

The fact that blueberries are continually promoted for their superfood credentials has never concerned me. The fact that they are delicious is what has me sold. Having a perfectly crisp blueberry burst in your mouth is a great pleasure. The best way to tell if blueberries are worth buying is to taste one and make sure it isn't floury. If it is, ditch it; floury blueberries are so disappointing.

I used to stop at the farmers' markets in Byron Bay as a kid and stock up on blueberries. The drive home was about two hours. There were never any left by the time we got back and I could never understand why I always had a tummy ache. A little bit addictive, methinks.

BLUEBERRIES

Blueberry verjus & coulis ◌

**MAKES 500 ML
(17 FL OZ/2 CUPS)**

BLUEBERRY VERJUS
250 g (9 oz) blueberries
   (2 punnets)
500 ml (17 fl oz) verjus
   (see page 218)

BLUEBERRY COULIS
blueberries (left over
   from the verjus)
Sugar syrup (page 217)

A variation on a recipe from my time at Restaurant Lûmé, a wildly creative tasting menu–driven restaurant where we created ten non-alcoholic pairings for an eighteen-course menu. So much of a drink is the perceived flavour based on its appearance, and the blueberries add an incredible colour. Appearance is normally the last thing on my mind when making a great cocktail – in fact, most of mine come out a strange shade of brown, so this is a welcome change. You'll need to start this recipe twelve hours ahead of time.

Start by freezing the blueberries. This both preserves the fruit and allows it to break down in the verjus.

Once frozen, combine the blueberries and the verjus. I like to do this in a sealable bag so that I can crush the fruit in the liquid. Leave to macerate for 12 hours, then strain and bottle the verjus, reserving the fruit. Store in the fridge for up to 2 weeks.

To make the blueberry coulis, add equal parts sugar syrup to the remaining fruit and simmer for 10 minutes over a medium–low heat. Store in a sterilised jar in the fridge for up to 1 week.

For another day

Blueberry coulis in your cold-brew coffee. It's a good play on a common tasting note in cold-brew coffee.

Spike your ginger beer. Increase the tartness of your ginger beer with a shot of blueberry verjus.

Blue cane

40 ml (1¼ fl oz) Blueberry
    verjus (page 55)
20 ml (¾ fl oz) Lemongrass
    syrup (page 217)
20 ml (¾ fl oz) virgin cane
    spirit
dash of pastis

Cane spirits come in many forms – agricole rhum, Cachaça or virgin cane spirit – depending on where in the world it is produced. They are made from fermenting sugar cane juice as opposed to molasses (as with rum). This produces a pure, vegetal-flavoured spirit. Blue drinks are rarely taken seriously, but this one should be.

Combine all the ingredients in a shaker and give it a solid shake. Strain into a coupette or cocktail glass, stick your little finger out and sip away.

B2Tea 💧

**MAKES 1 LARGE OR
2 REGULAR-SIZED
COCKTAILS**

45 ml (1½ fl oz) Blueberry
    verjus (page 55)
20 ml (¾ fl oz) Blueberry
    coulis (page 55)
45 ml (1½ fl oz) Black tea
    syrup (page 214)
60 ml (2 fl oz) soda water
    (club soda)
ice cubes, to serve
mint sprig, to garnish

Shaun and I always find ourselves going back to iced teas. Whenever we decide that a period of detoxing is required, tea is always the fallback to fill the void in a glass. This cocktail offers a great way to use blueberries in two forms: in the verjus and in the coulis.

Add the verjus, coulis and tea syrup to a serving glass, give it a stir, then splash with soda water. Fill with ice.

Give the mint sprig a light slap to awaken and freshen it, then garnish.

Blackberry

Blackberries are classically cool-climate, wild berries that grow on thorny bushes. They are a member of the rose family, so foraging for them is a scratchy affair. Also known as brambles, these berries have been used in classic French liqueurs (mure) and cocktails for a lot longer than I've been drinking. We use the Loch Ness variety (most commonly available) to make our Marionette Mure at Marionette.

Access to fresh blackberries was a rare treat growing up. They don't travel very well and the fresh fruit doesn't hold up in Queensland's summer heat. When they were available, they were a dinner party luxury, mixed with mint and icing sugar to dress desserts. Access to other varieties of blackberries, including loganberries, marion berries, silvan berries and boysenberries, was even rarer.

BOYSENBERRY

LOCH NESS

LOGANBERRY

MARION BERRY

SILVAN BERRY

SPRING   SUMMER   AUTUMN   WINTER

Spiced blackberry syrup

**MAKES APPROX. 500 ML
(17 FL OZ/2 CUPS)**

500 g (1 lb 2 oz)
   blackberries
250 g (9 oz) caster
   (superfine) sugar
½ cinnamon stick
½ star anise
3 cloves
a few gratings of fresh
   nutmeg

While blackberries are a summer fruit, they conjure warming winter spice flavours for me, and these classic spices pair so well with the dark fruit – the perfect foil for the acidity of the blackberry.

Combine all the ingredients in a saucepan with 1 litre (34 fl oz/ 4 cups) water. Set the pan over a medium heat and bring the mixture to the boil. Reduce the heat slightly and simmer for 30 minutes.

Strain through a fine-mesh sieve and pour the syrup into a sterilised glass bottle (see page 15). Compost the pulp. Store in the fridge for up to 2 weeks.

For another day

Mix with BBQ sauce. Perfect for a pork or chicken glaze.

Make a bedtime treat. Mix with hot chamomile tea (see page 214) for a soothing drink before bed.

Fill your sandwich. Mixed with peanut butter, this syrup makes a great sandwich filling.

Iced blackberry horchata

Night-market gluvine

45 ml (1½ fl oz) Spiced
  blackberry syrup
  (page 59)
100 ml (3½ fl oz) light
  red wine (see *Note*)

IF SERVING COLD
ice cubes, to serve
fresh blueberries, to
  garnish

Growing up, my mum and dad had friends in Germany who would send us a Christmas care package each year. The stollen and assortment of biscuits was a highlight of the festive period. These German festive hampers go hand-in-hand with Christmas night markets, which pop up all over the northern hemisphere during winter. I have been lucky enough to visit German night markets in Germany, Canada and England – even Australia, though of course these are usually held in mid July. The one constant pleasure of all these markets was the gluvine, or mulled wine.

Combine the ingredients in a mug and microwave on high for 30 seconds. Remove and stir, then microwave for another 30 seconds. Alternatively, warm in a saucepan over a low heat, stirring occasionally, for around 5 minutes.

You can also serve it cold for a crowd. Build five serves in a large jug over ice and garnish with fresh berries.

Something young and juicy, such as pinot noir, is ideal.

Iced blackberry horchata ◌

75 ml (2½ fl oz) Macadamia
  milk (page 203), or your
  choice of nut milk
60 ml (2 fl oz) cold-brew
  coffee (page 215)
30 ml (1 fl oz) Spiced
  blackberry syrup
  (page 59)
ice cubes, to serve
fresh nutmeg, to garnish

Horchata is a flavoured nut or rice milk drink from Mexico. We think that Spiced blackberry syrup plays with the creaminess of a nut milk very well. For this recipe, we have used our Macadamia milk, but for those who don't have the time to make it fresh, a good-quality, shop-bought nut milk works a treat. Serve as an iced-coffee alternative for morning tea.

Combine all the ingredients and give them a quick stir with some ice, either in individual cups or in a jug as a centrepiece. Grate a little nutmeg on top to garnish.

Currant

Currants come in red, white and black, the white being very delicate and hard to find. The red conjures memories of Christmas turkey, while the black takes us back to childhood memories of Ribena, and then on to lashings of cassis in kirs once you reached drinking age.

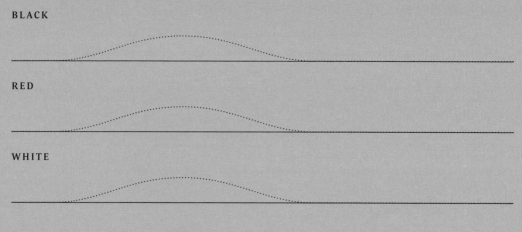

BLACK

RED

WHITE

SPRING   SUMMER   AUTUMN   WINTER

Currant jelly ⬗

**MAKES APPROX. 500 ML
(17 FL OZ/2 CUPS)**

1 kg (2 lb 3 oz) currants
 with stems
600 g (1 lb 5 oz) caster
 (superfine) sugar
juice of 1 lemon

This currant jelly draws inspiration from the family of the farmer that we get our currants from to make our cassis. The Clark family of Westerway Raspberry Farm rely on the jam-making recipes of Beryl Clark, the farmer's grandmother. This recipe was classically made with redcurrants, but works well with any variety.

Combine the currants with 100 ml (3½ fl oz) water in a saucepan over a medium heat, muddling as you go. Cook until the currants are soft, then pass them through a fine-mesh sieve. Reserve the liquid and compost the pulp.

Add the sugar and lemon juice to the liquid and cook over a high heat, stirring occasionally, for 30 minutes. To test if your jelly has reached setting point, place a small saucer in the freezer. Once cold, dollop a teaspoon of jelly onto the saucer, wait a few moments, then run your finger through the jelly. If it leaves a clean line, with no jelly leaking into the middle, it is ready. Transfer the jelly to sterilised glass jars (see page 15). Once jarred, it will keep for up to 6 months.

For another day

Jelly instead of jam. Mum used to add my grandma's jellies to a bread and butter pudding instead of jam, making for a fun surprise.

Winter warmer. Add it to warm cider for a winter tipple.

Passing thyme

100 ml (3½ fl oz)
  chardonnay
1 tablespoon Currant jelly
  (opposite)
dash of pastis
2 thyme sprigs
ice cubes, for shaking

Currants have quite a thick skin. When cooked, they produce an incredible savoury, green-tomato skin quality, as well as really grippy tannins – think adult Ribena – so adding a savoury edge works perfectly. We've used anise and thyme here to make a very fun, but very adult, mock rosé wine.

Combine all the ingredients with one of the thyme sprigs and shake away. Strain into a wine glass, then garnish with the remaining thyme sprig.

Not a kir in the world

90 ml (3 fl oz) verjus
  (see page 218)
1 tablespoon Currant jelly
  (page 64)
10 ml (¼ fl oz) Oak syrup
  (page 217)
ice cubes, for shaking
45 ml (1½ fl oz) soda water
  (club soda) (optional)

We have based this drink on the idea of the early kir cocktail. The story goes that Felix Kir, a priest who became the mayor of Burgundy, would throw lavish parties. At the time, aligote (a lesser-known white wine grape with high acidity) was in surplus, as everyone wanted to drink chardonnay. So, to use the excess wine and please the guests at the same time, Felix would add cassis (blackcurrant liqueur) to the wine – and the kir was born. This cocktail uses oak syrup to evoke the spice and richness of wine maturing in barrel.

Combine all the ingredients except the soda water with ice and try not to pull a strange face while you shake. Strain into a wine glass. With this drink, you have the option of drinking as is or adding a splash of soda water to lengthen and lift it slightly.

Grape

Grapes are funny things. The ones that make the best wines are often less desirable to eat.

Wine grapes, or *vitis vinifera*, are much sweeter than table grapes, which makes sense as they are fermented to make alcohol. Table grapes, *vitis labrusca*, have changed significantly over the course of my life from smaller, more tightly bunched berries with seeds to larger, seedless fruits. As people tend to shop with their eyes, the varieties that we see the most are the plump, seedless ones.

Fun fact: there are now some wines being made in Japan using table grapes. It's reminiscent of strong grape soda.

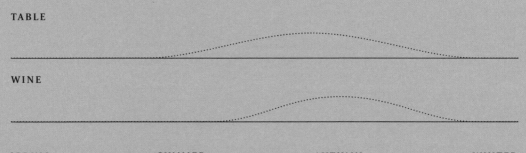

TABLE

WINE

SPRING   SUMMER   AUTUMN   WINTER

Aromatised grape juice

**MAKES 1 LITRE
(34 FL OZ/4 CUPS)**

2 kg (4 lb 6 oz) grapes
  of your choice
5 g (⅛ oz) tartaric acid
100 ml (3½ fl oz) gin
10 g (¼ oz) fresh
  wormwood leaves

This recipe came about when we were asked to help a friend feel included at a party. They were unable to drink alcohol, but didn't want to answer any questions, so we set to work. The recipe has evolved over the past four years, but it essentially began as a blend of muscat grape juice and tonic syrup. Here, you can sub in dried wormwood if you're unable to find fresh, but just halve the quantity. You'll need to start this recipe two days ahead of time.

Start by pressing the grapes, either using a juicer or with the end of a rolling pin.

Add the tartaric acid, gin and wormwood to the grape juice and stir to dissolve. If you used a juicer, add the grape skins and pulp back in, then leave to rest for 48 hours.

Strain the liquid through a fine-mesh sieve. The pulp and seeds can now be composted. Pour the juice into a sterilised glass bottle (see page 15), seal and refrigerate. It will keep for up to 2 weeks.

For another day

Mix with tonic water. It's a great, very low-ABV version of a vermouth and tonic.

Make a martini. Mix with a gin-like hydrosol in a 2:1 ratio for a martini.

Try a grape & grape. Mix equal parts grape juice with dry sherry.

Fronds

Fronds

60 ml (2 fl oz) Aromatised
   grape juice (page 67)
60 ml (2 fl oz)
   fresh-pressed apple
   juice
20 ml (¾ fl oz) aquavit
5 ml (⅛ fl oz) Sugar syrup
   (page 217)
3 fennel fronds
30 ml (1 fl oz) soda water
   (club soda)
ice cubes, to serve

Aquavit has a polarising flavour, with notes of dill and caraway that are both acquired tastes. It is something that confused me greatly until someone much wiser broke it down nice and simply: it's essentially a juniperless gin with a different spice. Funnily enough, this is all it took to convince me to use it.

Briefly shake the grape juice, apple juice, aquavit, sugar syrup and two of the fennel fronds. Strain into a highball glass, then top with soda water and fill with ice.

Drape the final fennel frond over the top to garnish.

Blushing swizzle

60 ml (2 fl oz) Aromatised
   grape juice (page 67)
60 ml (2 fl oz) sparkling
   apple juice
20 ml (¾ fl oz) grenadine
   (page 219)
3 dill sprigs
crushed ice, to serve

A swizzle is where you use a bar spoon or specially made stick to pull the ingredients up through crushed ice in a tropical-style drink. A personal favourite of mine is the Queen's park swizzle. Here, the addition of dill and grenadine gives a great colour contrast and really makes this swizzle sing. Draw the reds and greens up, as if you are trying to light a fire in Scouts.

Combine all the ingredients except the ice in a highball glass.

Top the drink with the crushed ice.

Using a bar spoon, fork or whatever is handy, spin and draw the ingredients up through the ice.

Tropical fruits

Tropical fruits are generally those that are grown closer to the equator. These environments have high temperatures and high humidity, producing perennial, evergreen crops.

For me, tropical fruits have always brought tiki drinks – long drinks with extravagant garnishes – and tropical shirts to mind. However, the real beauty of using tropical fruit it its accessibility. Being able to get crops of these fruits all year round is incredible.

Farmers rotate plantings, so that the harvest of fruit will be spaced out. It's a beautiful thing, especially as you venture closer to the equator and realise that there isn't really a winter, just seasons differing based on rainfall.

–Nick

Passionfruit

Nature's own dessert dressing. Scooped over fruit salad, spooned onto breakfast or cut open to enjoy as a snack, there's just no denying the versatility of the passionfruit. They are great for sharing too, as I always find half to be the perfect serving for one.

These beautiful little fruits are an ideal addition to classic, tiki-style cocktails, adding small bursts of flavour to drinks like the mojito or the hurricane. Reserve the husk for a pyrotechnic garnish on top. Just douse in rum and set alight.

In Brisbane, a passionfruit vine would climb the fence between us and our neighbours. It was the black variety that produced shriveled-up fruit. There are purple ones too – often lighter in colour and much plumper, with the pulp much more easily removed – but there's not much difference in flavour. It's funny, I never knew how much I enjoyed passionfruit and mangoes until they weren't there all the time. You know what they say ...

BLACK

PURPLE

SPRING   SUMMER   AUTUMN   WINTER

Passionfruit cordial ⬦

**MAKES 1 LITRE
(34 FL OZ/4 CUPS)**

10 passionfruit
500 g (1 lb 2 oz) caster
  (superfine) sugar
10 g (¼ oz) citric acid

I really like this recipe, as it is very true to the fruit – sharp, with all the beautiful acidic sweetness – but without the need to chew the pesky little seeds that are matted throughout.

Halve the passionfruit, scrape out the pulp and reserve. Add the husks to a saucepan with 1.5 litres (51 fl oz/6 cups) water and boil for 30 minutes, extracting as much residual pulp as possible. Strain off the husks and set aside (see *Note*).

To the liquid, add the reserved pulp, sugar and acid, then simmer in a pan for 10 minutes. Strain through a fine-mesh sieve and pour into a sterilised glass bottle (see page 15). The cordial will last for up to 2 weeks in the fridge.

Wash and set aside the halved husks for all your tiki garnish needs. I find it best to dehydrate them (see page 14) for a couple of days outside on a drying rack.

For another day

Use as a sweetener. Add to natural yoghurt or a smoothie.

Make a granita. Just add water and egg whites (see page 37).

Spice up your beer. Add a dash of cordial to your favourite wheat beer for an interesting flavour note.

Mrs Cohen's wall 💧

45 ml (1½ fl oz)
  unflavoured kombucha
20 ml (¾ fl oz) Passionfruit
  cordial (page 73)
20 ml (¾ fl oz) Coconut
  cream (page 82)
10 ml (¼ fl oz) Lemongrass
  syrup (page 217)
ice cubes, for shaking
dried passionfruit husk
  (see page 14), to garnish

Sally Cohen is a close family friend who used to babysit me and my siblings. She moved in next door to us, which I'm sure she went on to regret. We used to climb the fence to raid the passionfruit vine on her side, as we had already depleted the one on ours.

Combine all the ingredients in a shaker with ice. Shake hard and fast, then dump all the contents into a rocks glass.

Garnish with the dried passionfruit husk.

Charlie's pick-me-up

30 ml (1 fl oz) aged rum
30 ml (1 fl oz) Passionfruit
  cordial (page 73)
60 ml (2 fl oz) sparkling
  apple juice
ice cubes, to serve
2 mint sprigs, to garnish

Charlie was my boss at the fruit shop I worked at throughout university. Come four o'clock on a Sunday afternoon, he would be craving a bit of sugar to get him through the last couple of hours. While his drink never contained alcohol (that I was aware of), I'm sure he would have liked it better this way.

Combine the rum and passionfruit cordial in a highball glass and stir to mix well. Top with sparkling apple juice, then fill the glass with ice.

Give the mint a quick slap and stick it in the top.

Pineapple

Pineapples have long been associated with the hospitality industry. In fact, I would go so far as to say they are a symbol of hospitality and bartending.

Historically, being able to buy pineapples was a sign of wealth and prosperity, and it was rare for them to break down in transit as they were shipped across the world. They quickly found a home behind the bar too, as their sweet, acidic juice became the backbone of many fun and refreshing cocktails.

Visiting fruit markets, I was always confused as to why the pineapples were without their tops. It turns out that pineapples, bred to be sweet and highly acidic, had their tops removed so that they couldn't be replanted, thus protecting the farmers' prized fruits. Great for the farmer, but not so great for the customer; one easy way to test the ripeness of a pineapple is to pull out its leaves. Luckily, you can also tell by the smell. If they're sweet-smelling, you're good to go.

While there are numerous varieties around the world, we have broken them down into two categories: smooth and rough, referring to their leaves. The smooth is bred to be higher yielding in juice and often sweeter, and the rough more fibrous.

ROUGH

....

SMOOTH

....

SPRING   SUMMER   AUTUMN   WINTER

Tepache ◌

**MAKES 2 LITRES
(68 FL OZ/8 CUPS)**

2 pineapples, washed
200 g (7 oz) brown sugar
5 g (⅛ oz) cloves

Tepache is a fermented pineapple drink often sold by street vendors in Mexico. More and more bartenders are exploring fermentation and becoming more creative, so these traditional fermented drinks are slowly making their way around the world.

The process of fermentation (the conversion of yeast and sugar into carbon dioxide and alcohol) will yield low levels of alcohol (less than 2 per cent) and add a yeasty, slightly sour finish to the drink. You will need to start this recipe three days ahead of time.

Start by cutting the pineapple into 3 cm (1¼ in) wedges (as you might for a fruit platter); you don't need to remove the skin. If there are leaves, twist them to remove and set them aside to garnish drinks or plant in the backyard.

Heat 2 litres (68 fl oz/8 cups) water in a saucepan over a medium heat and add the sugar. Stir until dissolved, then add the cloves.

Put the pineapple cubes in a large sterilised container and pour over the sugar syrup. Cover with a piece of muslin (cheesecloth) and leave on the kitchen bench for 3 days.

Pass the liquid through a fine-mesh sieve and store in an airtight container in the fridge. Compost the pineapple chunks. The tepache will keep for up to 2 weeks in the fridge.

For another day

Great mixed with any vegetal spirit. Try an unaged cane spirit or agave spirit, depending on what is local to you.

Drink as is. Over ice, or with a splash of soda water (club soda).

Turn it into a vinegar. See page 17.

A tickle in the throat

60 ml (2 fl oz) Tepache
(page 77)
30 ml (1 fl oz) peated
whisky
1 teaspoon honey
3 cracks of black pepper
ice cubes, for shaking

A tickle in the throat is just as it sounds – equally refreshing and grown up. The smoky whisky mildly curbs the acidic tickle of the pineapple tepache as it goes down. It feels almost medicinal, really.

Combine all the ingredients in a shaker with ice and shake hard and fast – really use some elbow grease. Dump all the contents into a rocks glass and happy days!

On a hot summer's night

60 ml (2 fl oz) Coconut
water (page 82)
60 ml (2 fl oz) Tepache
(page 77)
60 ml (2 fl oz) cold-brew
black tea (page 214),
such as lapsang
souchong
ice cubes, to serve
2 coriander (cilantro)
sprigs, to garnish

There is something quite soothing about coconut water. Maybe it's the electrolyte boost. Maybe it's the luxurious coconut fats that coat the walls of your mouth. While this drink works with any black tea, the one we like to play with is a lapsang souchong; the smoky black tea flavour adds a real toasty element to the drink. It's kind of like barbecued pineapple. Yum!

Combine the coconut water, tepache and tea over ice in a highball glass. Stir to combine, then allow the coriander to lounge over the top.

Coconut

Coconuts come in different shapes, sizes and colours. The palms are found around the tropics and are broken into two categories: those that fertilise themselves and those that cross-fertilise. The main difference is the coconut's husk, or exterior. The classic image of brown nuts high up on a tree on a deserted island is not always the case.

Softer-husk plants are often cultivated for their liquid, while the harder varieties are famed for their flesh.

We are going to treat them in the same manner, as it is not common to find both in the same area, and we always need to work with what we have at our fingertips.

COCONUT

Coconut water, milk & cream

**MAKES 150 ML
(5 FL OZ) COCONUT
WATER,
300 ML (10 FL OZ)
COCONUT MILK &
150 ML (5 FL OZ)
COCONUT CREAM**

1 coconut
300 ml (10 fl oz) hot water

This is how to extract all the components of the coconut to maximise its uses. The idea is to create different textures and flavours that can all be used in slightly different ways. It requires some unconventional tools, but you should have them lying around in your garden shed. I find a hammer and chisel to be the most effective. You'll need to start this recipe two hours ahead of time.

Holding the coconut steady with a tea towel (dish towel), gently hit it with a hammer, rotating the coconut until it splits. Make sure you only go as far as cracking it so that you can drain the water (don't break it open completely).

Drain off the coconut water and set aside, then give it a few more whacks to break up the shell. Now, carefully, using a (clean) chisel, separate the white flesh from the brown husk. In a food processor, blitz all the flesh into fine pieces. Add the hot water and blitz again. Pass the coconut through a fine-mesh sieve. Leave to sit in the fridge for 2 hours. The cream will sit on top and the milk will sink to the bottom. To separate, simply scrape the cream off the top.

Set aside the pulp, dry it out or toast it in the oven and use to texture a fantastic chicken salad.

All three elements will last for 3 days in the fridge.

If you are short on time, you can use desiccated coconut mixed with water to make just the coconut milk. Use 50 g (1¾oz) coconut to every 300 ml (10 fl oz) water.

For another day

Make an afternoon cooler. Combine coconut water with Mango vermouth (page 115) over ice.

For dessert. Serve coconut cream with Banana caramel (page 85) on top of your tapioca pudding.

Spice it up. Use the cream and milk for stirring into curries.

A good alternative. Use coconut milk instead of dairy milk for those with lactose intolerances.

Half-time beer

40 ml (1¼ fl oz) Coconut
milk (page 82)
20 ml (¾ fl oz) Sugar syrup
(page 217)
150 ml (5 fl oz) Gose beer
(see *Note*)
pinch of Smoked thyme
salt (page 181), to garnish

During a demanding restaurant or bar service, there is nothing
more refreshing, relaxing and reaffirming for the team than to
share a half-time beer (one between three, to be responsible).
A small splash of alcohol calms the nerves and the cold bubbles
instantly cool your temper, not to mention that the brief pause
makes you realise everything is under control and will be alright.

A Gose is a briny style of beer, great for such an occasion due
to its generally low alcohol content. In this recipe, we mix it up
in a tropical fusion.

Combine the coconut milk and sugar syrup in a chilled beer glass
and stir to combine. Add a splash of the beer, then stir again.
Slowly top with the rest of the beer to avoid it bubbling over.

Sprinkle with a pinch of thyme salt to garnish. Bob's your uncle:
the perfect half-time quencher.

I like to use a beer with a fruit element.

Internal combustion

40 ml (1¼ fl oz) Coconut
cream (page 82)
30 ml (1 fl oz) Kaffir lime
syrup (page 217)
20 ml (¾ fl oz) tamarind
purée (see *Note*)
15 ml (½ fl oz) ginger juice
ice cubes, for shaking
kaffir lime leaf, to garnish

If a coconut is left to its own devices for long enough in the heat
of summer, there will be quite a mess to clean up. The internal
fermentation of the flesh will build pressure within the coconut and
it will eventually pop, spreading creamy coconut flesh everywhere.
This drink has a fantastic tropical aroma, similar to that of a freshly
popped coconut.

Combine all the ingredients in a shaker with ice. Give it a hard
shake, then strain into a cocktail glass. Gently sit the kaffir lime
leaf on top.

You will find tamarind purée in your local Asian supermarket.

Banana

Even now, when I walk past bananas in a supermarket, it is hard not to start humming 'Banana - na - na - na, make those bodies sing!', the hook for a catchy advertisement that played on Australian screens in the mid-to-late nineties. Technically a berry, bananas are synonymous with tropical parts of the world. The further north you drive in Australia, big blue or silver sleeping bags can be seen hanging from the palms. These are used to protect the bananas from the elements and hungry wildlife, and you really know you're in the north of Australia when you see them.

Bananas are also the simplest of snacks: packaged for convenience and accessible to all. They are great on cereal, with yoghurt or just on their own, and I have started the day with them for as long as I can remember. Even once they have begun to turn brown and sickly sweet, bananas still find their uses, particularly in banana bread, which is almost guaranteed not to make it off the cooling rack before being devoured.

The most common variety of banana is the Cavendish, but most of the time you'll notice there isn't a label on your fruit. Lady fingers are also fairly readily available; they are a shorter and slightly sweeter fruit but, for all intents and purposes, they are still a regular banana – just smaller.

CAVENDISH

LADY FINGER

Banana caramel

**MAKES 200 ML
(7 FL OZ)**

400 g (14 oz/1¾ cups)
  caster (superfine) sugar
4 bananas, peeled
  and chopped (peels
  reserved; see *Note*)
150 ml (5 fl oz) pouring
  (single/light) cream
5 g (⅛ oz) salt

A banana flavour is quite an elusive one to capture in liquid form; however, this luxurious recipe does it really well, and it's ideal for special occasions or for eating straight out of the fridge, Nigella-style, when late-night cravings call.

Combine the sugar with 200 ml (7 fl oz) water in a saucepan over a medium heat. Stir until dissolved, then cook, without stirring, until the sugar begins to caramelise.

Add the banana and cook for a further 15 minutes, without stirring, until it darkens. Remove from the heat and add the cream, being careful as it will bubble and spit. Stir to homogenise, then force the mixture through a fine-mesh sieve to remove the banana pulp (reserve for adding to breakfasts or desserts, or freeze in ice-cube trays to make smoothie cubes).

Transfer to a sterilised glass jar (see page 15), seal, then allow to cool before refrigerating. It will keep for up to 2 weeks.

Both my mum and grandma always encouraged me to eat more bananas so they could feed the tree ferns with the peels; staghorn ferns break down the minerals in the organic banana peel. Grandma loved that they added a tropical feel to her quite dry garden.

For another day

Use it for layering. Stick it in a pavlova, Eton mess or banana split.

Drizzle. Pour some over your favourite biscuit.

Go Vietnamese. Use it in Vietnamese-style coffee (in place of condensed milk), or in iced coffee.

Upping the milkshake game

30 ml (1 fl oz) **Banana caramel (page 85)**
10 ml (¼ fl oz) **dark molasses**
45 ml (1½ fl oz) **full-cream (whole) milk**
1 tablespoon **Greek or natural yoghurt**
1 teaspoon **cocoa powder**
1 teaspoon **malted milk powder**
ice cubes, to serve

Who doesn't love a banana milkshake or smoothie? This lands somewhere in the middle: a little adult, with the bitterness of the cocoa and molasses, but with all the youthful exuberance of a banana lolly (sweet) on top of a neon-coloured shake.

Shake all the ingredients together and pour over ice, or blitz everything in a food processor – whatever is on hand.

Serve over ice in a highball glass or milkshake tin. Add a metal straw if you have one for some retro-diner (and environmentally friendly) charm.

Banana refashioned

20 ml (¾ fl oz) **Banana caramel (page 85)**
20 ml (¾ fl oz) **muscat**
20 ml (¾ fl oz) **dark rum**
20 ml (¾ fl oz) **cold-brew black tea (page 214)**
ice cubes, for stirring
piece of rock ice, to serve
orange twist, to garnish

This is a fun, responsible take on an old fashioned that plays on the rich oak flavour of classic aged spirits, such as rum or whisky. The sticky, mature fruit of the muscat works so well with the tannins of the tea. The effect is best achieved by allowing the tea to sit for a little bit too long, over-extracting and building the tannins that will grip the inside of your cheeks as you drink.

Combine all the ingredients and stir over ice (just a short stir, as you are not looking to dilute the drink very much).

Strain over a large piece of rock ice and dress with an orange twist.

Papaya

Papaya is one of those fruits that, for me, needs to be perfectly ripe or it is just not enjoyable; it's a combination of the strong smell and texture of the fruit. If it's underripe, its gritty. If it's overripe, it turns to mush. Just right, though, and it's tropical bliss. The problem is that when you do find that perfectly ripe fruit, it's usually the one that a toddler has prodded and broken the skin of (a good sign that it's ready to go).

Here in Australia, the classic papaya is called a Hawaiian or red paw paw, while the yellow papaya is just referred to as a paw paw. The yellow-fleshed fruit is sweeter, but also has a more pronounced aroma, while the red-fleshed fruit is subtler and holds up on a fruit plate for much longer.

HAWAIIAN/RED
....

YELLOW/PAW PAW
....

SPRING   SUMMER   AUTUMN   WINTER

Papaya lassi ◌

**MAKES 1 LITRE
(34 FL OZ/4 CUPS)**

1 papaya
250 g (9 oz/1 cup) natural
  yoghurt
10 g (¼ oz) citric acid
10 ml (¼ fl oz) honey
pinch of salt

A lassi is classically an Indian yoghurt-based drink, served as an accompaniment to a curry. It's normally a spiced drink with cardamom, cumin and salt. However, a touch of honey gives it a fantastic lift. Personally, I like a lassi as a banana smoothie alternative in the morning.

Halve the papaya and scrape out the seeds. Remove the skin (see *Note*).

Add the flesh of the papaya and the rest of the ingredients to a food processor with 500 ml (17 fl oz/2 cups) water and blitz. The lassi will keep in the fridge for up to 3 days in an airtight container.

Put the skins aside and use them to flavour a tropical iced tea (page 214), or to add flavour to your next batch of vinegars (see page 17).

For another day

Serve with poppadoms. Or to relieve the heat of your favourite curry.

Add a tropical crunch. Scrape out the seeds and add them to a jar of honey for a couple of days to add a tropical touch to your bircher muesli.

Add coconut rum. Everyone has their guilty pleasure when it comes to alcohol. Coconut rum is definitely mine (to keep it fair, Shaun's is a whisky cream liqueur).

Coconuts in the well 💧

60 ml (2 fl oz) Papaya lassi
   (opposite)
60 ml (2 fl oz) Coconut
   water (page 82)
ice cubes, to serve
1 mint sprig
dash of hot sauce, to serve
   (optional)

This cocktail is a terrible reference to Lassie the dog's informative barks about somebody having fallen into a well. (Naming drinks has never really been my strong suit.) The cocktail is good, though – the perfect quick pick-me-up: fresh, healthy and invigorating.

Combine the papaya lassi and coconut water in a tall glass over ice. Give it a quick stir and whack the mint sprig in for a fresh lift.

If you like a little spice, serve with a dash of hot sauce.

Colombo day spa

90 ml (3 fl oz) Papaya lassi
   (opposite)
30 ml (1 fl oz) white rum
dash of absinthe
ice cubes, for shaking
pinch of smoked paprika,
   to garnish

Colombo has become a destination for pampering, with day spas and clubs aplenty. And, while it might be a dreary, rain-sodden afternoon wherever you are, we all love to dream of putting our feet up, feeling exotic and relaxing in a palm-laden paradise. This drink will get you halfway there.

Combine the lassi, rum and absinthe in a shaker with ice. Shake hard and fast, then strain into a cocktail glass.

Add a small pinch of smoked paprika to garnish. To get a nice, even spread, I like to put the pinch of paprika into a tea strainer and dust it over the top.

Stone fruits

Also known as drupe fruits, these wonderful edibles contain, as you would guess, a stone (pit) in the middle. There are two kinds: clingstone, where the flesh really holds onto the fruit, and freestone, where the stone is easier to remove.

Stone fruits, for me, have always been a sign of summer, even if some varieties skirt the edges of the season. In Australia, it wouldn't be Christmas without cherries on the table, and ditto the Boxing Day Test without mangoes.

One of the big centres for stone fruit in Australia is the Goulburn Valley, which has had some difficulties in recent years. The first was the closure of a large processing/canning factory in the area. The second concerned issues with what supermarkets deemed fit to sell. For example, if there were any blemishes on the fruit (which can happen due to hail during the growing season), the supermarkets refused to accept it, regardless of its flavour. One day, Nick visited our apricot farmer and he was throwing out 2500 kilograms (more than 5500 pounds) of peaches because they were rejected by his supermarket client. Nick said they were some of the best peaches he had ever had. For this wasteful process to change, it's up to consumers to demand imperfect but natural fruit and veg.

One last thing: we often like to use the whole fruit, including the seeds and kernels, because it really does add an extra element, and it's excellent from a sustainability perspective. The only drawback with this approach is that some recipes in this chapter invite you to use parts of the fruit that contain small amounts of amygdalin. When ingested, amygdalin is converted into cyanide. While we have never experienced any ill-effects, and there is little-to-no evidence of risk, do be aware – and remember, less is more. If you prefer, each recipe can be made without these elements.

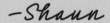

Apricot

When I was a kid, our neighbours across the road had an apricot tree. Actually, they had a whole veggie patch, but it was the apricots I was most interested in. During summer break, I would knock on their door to see if I could grab a couple. This happened daily and, if the neighbours weren't home, I would jump the fence and help myself!

There are many varieties of apricots, with the season starting in late spring and continuing through to late summer. There are tarter varieties and sweeter ones, but I am particularly fond of Castlebrites, which, while quite sweet, have a certain tang, and Moorparks, which are just so sweet off the tree, especially if picked a little late.

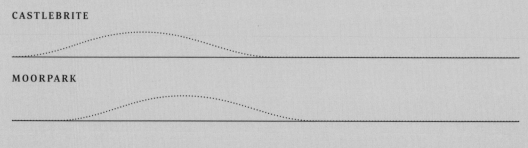

CASTLEBRITE

MOORPARK

SPRING SUMMER AUTUMN WINTER

Apricot jam 💧

**MAKES APPROX. 2 KG
(4 LB 6 OZ)**

1.5 kg (3 lb 5 oz) apricots
1 kg (2 lb 3 oz) caster
 (superfine) sugar
30 ml (1 fl oz) lemon juice

Jams are really easy to make and one of the best ways to use up a glut of fruit to ensure that you can enjoy it throughout the year. This recipe comes from Nick's grandma and, I must say, it is as good as it gets. You will need to start this recipe the night before you want to eat it.

Stone the apricots (reserving six stones to extract the kernels, if desired), then put the fruit in a bowl, cover with half the sugar and leave to macerate overnight.

If you want to use the kernels (see *Note*), crack the stones with a nutcracker to retrieve the kernels. Blanch them in a saucepan of boiling water for 5 minutes, then remove and peel off the skins. Allow to dry overnight.

The next day, place the macerated fruit in a large saucepan and add 250 ml (8½ fl oz/1 cup) water and the lemon juice. Simmer over a medium heat until the fruit is soft. Add the remaining sugar and blanched apricot kernels, if using. To test if your jam has reached setting point, place a small saucer in the freezer. Once cold, dollop a teaspoon of jam onto the saucer, wait a few moments, then run your finger through the jam. If it leaves a clean line with no jam leaking into the middle, it's ready. While the jam is hot, transfer it to sterilised glass jars (see page 15) and seal. Store for up to 6 months (and be sure to refrigerate after opening).

A quick note on apricot kernels – they do contain a small amount of amygdalin (see page 93), so feel free to leave them out if you'd prefer.

For another day

Yoghurt. Regardless of how you say it, yog-hurt or yo-ghurt, a scoop of apricot jam is a welcome addition! (For the record, I say yog-hurt.)

Morning toast. Is there a better way to start the day?

Old fashioned. The classic old fashioned requires four ingredients: spirit, sugar, water (ice) and bitters. Try subbing out the sugar for jam next time you whip one up.

Amaretto apricot flip

20 ml (¾ fl oz) amaretto
15 ml (½ fl oz) dessert wine
1 tablespoon Apricot jam
   (page 95)
1 egg yolk
2 dashes of aromatic
   bitters
ice cubes, for shaking
smoked almonds, to serve

If you haven't scooped apricot jam into custard, you haven't lived a full life, my friend. This is where the inspiration for this cocktail came from: using a whole egg yolk with a scoop of jam. The amaretto works well because a lot of brands on the market use apricot kernels in their production (see page 93). The dessert wine gives it a little acidic balance along with a crisp sweetness.

Shake all the ingredients with ice as hard as you can – the harder the better. Strain into a small wine glass and serve with some smoked almonds (I have been known to call them bacon nuts).

Apricot chai tea ◌

MAKES 2 SMALL CUPS
(OR 1 LARGE IF YOU'RE
THIRSTY LIKE ME)

2 tablespoons Apricot jam
   (page 95)
5 cloves
5 green cardamom pods
1 small cinnamon stick
10 g (¼ oz) brown sugar

I'm not sure when chai tea became popular in Australia, but it seemed almost overnight that every cafe started stocking their own chai blends. The common flavours found in those blends were cardamom, cinnamon and clove, among others. These spices work really well with apricots – well, cooked apricots, when those sugars have started to caramelise. And, since apricot jam is cooked apricots, it seemed perfect to mix up the jam with these spices.

Combine all the ingredients in a saucepan with 300 ml (10 fl oz) water and heat gently over a low heat for 7 minutes.

Strain into two cups. Drink and go to bed.

Peach

My favourite type of peach is the donut peach. I like both donuts and peaches, so the combination of the two was always going to work, right? Unfortunately, the name refers to the shape rather than the taste; however, the taste is also delightful.

Peaches generally fall into two categories: yellow and white. The yellows are generally richer, whereas the whites are more delicate and floral. Both are great. Nectarines also fall into the peaches camp, and these smooth-skinned cousins also come in white and yellow varieties.

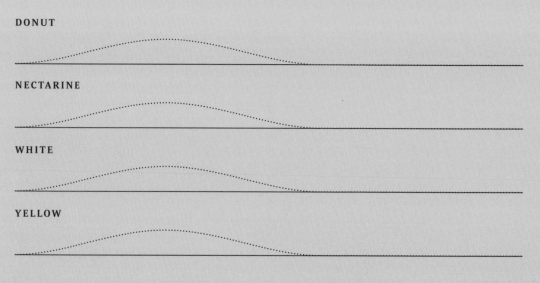

DONUT

NECTARINE

WHITE

YELLOW

SPRING   SUMMER   AUTUMN   WINTER

Peach liqueur

**MAKES APPROX. 750 ML
(25½ FL OZ/3 CUPS)**

5 peaches
500 ml (17 fl oz/2 cups)
  fortified white wine
  (something similar to
  white port)
250 g (9 oz) caster
  (superfine) sugar
100 ml (3½ fl oz) gin

A peach liqueur ensures that you can enjoy the flavour of peaches well past their season. We decided to use fortified white wine as the bulking agent here, as peaches are a common tasting note in this category. Also, fortified white wine is a lot lower in alcohol than gin, and lower alcohol is the sustainable approach. You'll need to start this recipe one week ahead of time.

Stone the peaches, reserving the stones to extract the kernels, if desired (see *Note*).

Muddle the fruit and mix it with the wine. Let it sit in an airtight container in the fridge for 1 week.

Strain the wine, pressing the peaches through a fine-mesh sieve to extract all the port. Add the fruit pulp to a saucepan with the sugar and 250 ml (8½ fl oz/1 cup) water. Bring to the boil over a medium–high heat and simmer for 30 minutes.

Strain the liquid through a fine-mesh sieve and combine it with the peach wine, then mix in the gin. Strain the liquid once more through a piece of muslin (cheesecloth), then pour into a sterilised glass bottle (see page 15). Set aside any leftover peach 'compôte' to make a cobbler or crumble.

This liqueur will last for up to 3 months in the fridge.

Peach kernels, like apricots, also contain amygdalin, so remember to use at your discretion (see page 93). We use them by blanching two kernels as described on page 95, then soaking them in the gin for a week. Strain off before using the gin.

For another day

Custard. Add just a touch of custard for a kick that's peachy.

Sake. One part liqueur to three parts sake on the rocks.

Rosewater & peaches

Peach bamboo

30 ml (1 fl oz) Peach
  liqueur (page 99)
30 ml (1 fl oz) dry
  vermouth
ice cubes, to serve
2 dashes of Orange bitters
  (page 42)
rosemary sprig, to garnish

There is a classic cocktail called a bamboo, which is a pleasant
blend of dry vermouth and dry sherry with a touch of sugar and
a drizzle of bitters. Here, we have swapped out the dry sherry for
the peach liqueur and omitted the sherry.

Add the liqueur and vermouth to an old fashioned glass. Top with
ice cubes and stir to dilute.

Finish with the bitters and garnish with a rosemary sprig. Drink,
then eat dinner, then make another one to digest.

Rosewater & peaches

**MAKES 1 COCKTAIL
OR PUNCH FOR 4
(SEE *NOTE*)**

50 ml (1¾ fl oz) Peach
  liqueur (page 99)
50 ml (1¾ fl oz) freshly
  squeezed orange juice
dash of rosewater
50 ml (1¾ fl oz) lemonade
  (lemon soda)
ice cubes, to serve
fresh rose petals, to
  garnish

Not a very inventive name, I know, but it gets the point across.
Rosewater is made two different ways, one of which you can do at
home by soaking roses petals in water. The other method involves
distillation techniques to produce a hydrosol. This can still be done
at home, but it's not as easy. You can make this recipe as a single
serve, or it also makes a great punch served in a jug on a warm day
in the rose garden. For this, you'll need a 2 litre (68 fl oz/8 cup) jug.

Combine the liqueur, orange juice and rosewater in a glass, or a jug
if you're making punch (see *Note*). Top with lemonade, then gently
add ice.

Garnish with (and smell) the roses ...

*To serve as a punch, make six times the quantity: use 300 ml each
of Peach liqueur, orange juice and lemonade, and 5 ml (⅛ fl oz) of
rosewater.*

Plum

What I love most about plums, besides the taste, is the variety of colours they come in. Greengages are green, damsons are purple and mirabelles are orange, and that's only skimming the surface. Their flavours are also quite different; mirabelles are rich and full, damsons a little astringent and tart, while greengages have a lovely honeyed sweetness about them. Something else I adore about plums is how the trees look when they're flowering; if you don't know the location of a tree, or it's the middle of winter, look it up and you'll see what I mean.

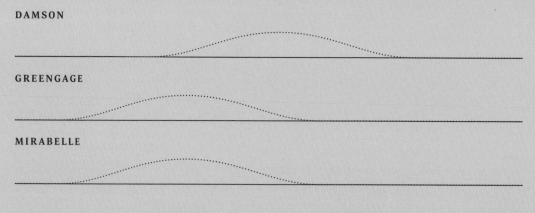

DAMSON

GREENGAGE

MIRABELLE

SPRING   SUMMER   AUTUMN   WINTER

Plum wine

**MAKES APPROX. 600 ML
(20½ FL OZ)**

5 plums
500 ml (17 fl oz/2 cups)
  sake
50 g (1¾ oz) rock sugar
  (substitute with caster/
  superfine sugar if
  need be)
200 ml (7 fl oz) hot water
5 prunes, roughly chopped

I've made this wine for the last two summers. The first one I made was with damsons and the second year I used greengages. They were both good, but I think the extra sweetness in the greengages was the better of the two. Prunes are nothing more than dried plums. You can buy them at the supermarket or you can do what I do and dry plums out at home. A dehydrator or low-temperature oven works just fine (see page 14). Just make sure to halve the plums and remove the stones first. You'll need to start this recipe one week ahead of time.

Halve the plums, remove the stones and slice the fruit into wedges. Add to the sake and store in an airtight container in the fridge for 1 week.

Strain the sake and set aside. Dehydrate the plums to use later as garnishes.

Combine the sugar and water in a saucepan over a medium heat, stirring to dissolve the sugar. Add the prunes and bring to the boil for 10 minutes. Strain, then leave the syrup to cool. Compost the prunes.

Combine the prune syrup with the plum sake and strain again, then pour into a sterilised glass bottle (see page 15). The plum wine will last for up to 1 week in the fridge.

For another day

Soda. Dilute the liqueur with soda water (club soda) for a refreshing beverage.

Prosecco. Spike your prosecco with plummy goodness.

Whisky highball. Basically a whisky and soda, but replace half the whisky with plum wine.

Plum(b) tuckered out

90 ml (3 fl oz) Macadamia
milk (page 203), or nut
milk of your choice
30 ml (1 fl oz) Plum wine
(page 103)
10 ml (¼ fl oz) brandy
5 ml (⅛ fl oz) Honey syrup
(page 218)
ice cubes, to serve
2 dashes of aromatic
bitters
dehydrated plums (see
page 14), to garnish

My dad used to say he was plumb tuckered out after a big week at work. I always used to think it was plum, not plumb. I didn't know it was the latter until I was writing this book. Moving on from that embarrassing fact, this drink is the perfect way to wind down from a hard day. You can use any nut milk you like, but I would recommend using our Macadamia milk.

Add all the ingredients except the bitters to a highball glass. Stir to combine, then top with ice.

Finish with the bitters and garnish with the dehydrated plum. Relax.

Drunken maesil cha

30 ml (1 fl oz) Plum wine
(page 103)
90 ml (3 fl oz) Iced green
tea (page 214)
5 ml (⅛ fl oz) Tonic syrup
(page 219)
30 ml (1 fl oz) soda water
(club soda)
ice cubes, to serve
dash of peated whisky
dehydrated plum (see
page 14), to garnish

Maesil cha is a traditional Korean fruit tea made from a green plum extract and, in some cases, smoked plums. That's where the inspiration for this drink started, even if it didn't finish anywhere near the original. The smoked component comes from just a touch of peated whisky, and even though maesil cha doesn't actually contain tea as the name suggests, green tea and plum work really well together.

Add the wine, tea and tonic syrup to a highball glass. Gently add the soda water and softly add ice. Float the whisky by pouring it on top of the drink, then garnish with the dehydrated plum.

Plum(b) tuckered out

Cherry

Growing up in Australia, I knew that Christmas was approaching when cherries started appearing in the fruit bowl, and that meant one thing: presents. I'm not sure if I enjoyed the cherries because of this or because of their flavour but, nonetheless, I still enjoy them today. I like to look at cherries as two distinct types: the sweet ones and the sour ones. Generally, the sour ones take a bit of work in the kitchen to get them up to spec' and really need to be used in things like jams, jellies, pies and preserves. Sweet cherries, on the other hand, are best when you eat them as close to the tree as possible.

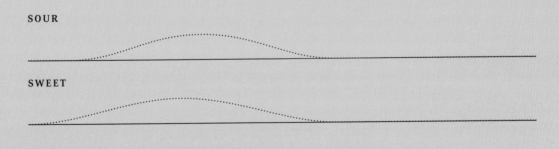

SOUR

SWEET

SPRING   SUMMER   AUTUMN   WINTER

Preserved cherries & syrup

**MAKES APPROX. 1 KG
(2 LB 3 OZ) OF MOREISH
PRESERVED CHERRIES**

20 g (¾ oz) cascara
  (see *Notes*)
1 kg (2 lb 3 oz) cherries
500 g (1 lb 2 oz) caster
  (superfine) sugar
100 ml (3½ fl oz) brandy
  (the older the better)

If you are using sweet cherries for this recipe, I would cut back on the sugar a little, maybe by 100 g (3½ oz), unless you have quite the sweet tooth. The great thing about making preserved cherries is not only that you get to enjoy cherries outside their season, but that the syrup is also great in drinks. Add a little soda water (club soda) or pour it over ice cream. You'll need to start this recipe one month ahead of time.

Combine the cascara with 350 ml (12 fl oz) water and refrigerate overnight.

Wash and pit the cherries (see *Notes*), then place them inside a sterilised glass jar (see page 15). Strain off the cascara and combine the liquid with the sugar in a saucepan. Bring to the boil and stir until the sugar has dissolved.

Pour the syrup and brandy over the cherries, seal, and leave to sit for 1 month before using. The cherries will last for up to 6 months in the fridge.

An interesting ingredient here is cascara, which is the dried husk of the coffee bean. It is usually discarded but it shouldn't be, as it's delightful. You can find it at good coffee roasters, but if you can't find it, fear not; the recipe will work without it, but it won't be quite as good unfortunately.

You can reserve the cherry pits to make cherry pit brandy (which is what we used for this recipe), but do remember that the pits contain amygdalin (see page 93). If, however, you do make it, you'll need about five pits to every 100 ml (3½ fl oz). Leave the brandy to sit for about 1 week before using.

For another day

Ice cream. Simply pour over ice cream. It's even better over a banana split.

Coconut water. Spike your coconut water with syrup – about a 1:5 cherry to coconut water ratio should do it.

Cherry chocolate milkshake

60 ml (2 fl oz) full-cream
(whole) milk
30 ml (1 fl oz) Cherry syrup
(opposite)
30 ml (1 fl oz) Cacao syrup
(page 217)
scoop of ice cream (the
larger the scoop, the
thicker the milkshake)
1 tablespoon malted milk
powder
Preserved cherries
(opposite), to garnish

My first job was at the Pancake Parlour, an Australian chain restaurant. One of the most popular drinks, besides spiders/floats (ice cream in soft drink – they're strangely good), was their milkshake dubbed the Swiss Mountain Malt. This was a rich shake made with ice cream and malted milk powder along with cream, milk and a flavoured syrup. I can't remember if there was a cherry flavour, but the syrup from the preserved cherries is a perfect addition here.

Combine all the ingredients in a blender and blitz until smooth.

Pour into a milkshake glass and garnish with preserved cherries. Drink through a crazy straw for maximum nostalgia.

Reverse cherry martini

5 Preserved cherries
(opposite), plus 1 extra
to garnish
45 ml (1½ fl oz) sweet
vermouth
15 ml (½ fl oz) gin
5 ml (⅛ fl oz) Citric
solution (page 216)
ice cubes, for stirring

There's a cocktail that I adore called a reverse or upside-down martini. It's basically a little bit of gin and a lot of vermouth – reverse measures of what was being drunk at the time it was invented. I once heard that Julia Child drank this cocktail in between drinking fancy French red wines to refresh her palate. Not sure if that is true, but it's a great story nonetheless.

Add the cherries to a mixing glass and muddle with a muddler or a rolling pin. Add the remaining ingredients with ice. Stir to dilute and chill, then strain into a cocktail glass through a double strainer or tea strainer.

Garnish with a preserved cherry. Enjoy your horrible drink (don't forget it's a *reverse* cocktail).

Lychee

Of all soapberries, I am the most familiar with the lychee. I have had rambutans (which I now prefer) and longan (which are okay), but the lychee is what I know from working in bars. Tinned lychees are stocked in a lot of bars where the preserved fruit is muddled into lychee martinis and the syrup mixed into lychee sours. I have never really liked tinned lychees. I don't think I ever will. It wasn't until I worked at Gin Palace that I discovered fresh lychees and fell in love. I started ordering kilos and kilos of them each week. I would even keep them in my top pocket while behind the bar so I had some on hand for those lychee martinis, or just whenever I wanted a quick snack. Ahh, those were the days – pocket lychees for everyone!

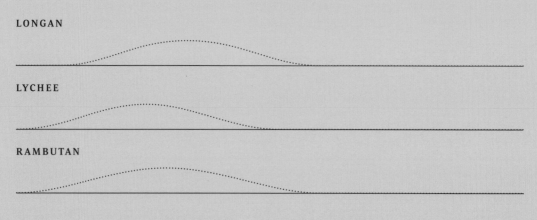

LONGAN

LYCHEE

RAMBUTAN

SPRING   SUMMER   AUTUMN   WINTER

Lychee vinegar ⬙

**MAKES APPROX. 1 LITRE
(34 FL OZ/4 CUPS)**

200 g (7 oz) raw honey
1 kg (2 lb 3 oz) lychees
1 vinegar mother
(see *Note*)

This recipe comes to us via a buddy of Nick's, chef Mike Layfield, who he worked with during his stint at Lûmé. Mike was in charge of all things fermented at the restaurant and has since moved on to start Felds Farm with his wife, Lauren, just outside of Hobart. Lychee and vinegar are a match made in heaven; the sweet, floral flavours of the lychee are brought back by the funky tartness of the vinegar. You'll need to start this recipe about six weeks ahead.

Combine the honey with 800 ml (27 fl oz) water in a saucepan and heat over a low heat to combine.

Crush the lychees in a sterilised preserving jar (see page 15) and pour the honey water on top. Cover with a piece of muslin (cheesecloth) and leave to ferment for 2 weeks (or until it has stopped bubbling). Strain into a clean glass jar and add the vinegar mother. Seal and leave to sit for a further 4 weeks to allow the alcohol to turn into vinegar. Compost your lychees. The vinegar will last for up to 6 months.

You can buy vinegar mothers at health-food stores.

For another day

Salad dressing. Mix equal parts lychee vinegar, oil and lemon.

Make lychee lemonade (lemon soda). Add just a splash.

Tropical fruit salad. Mix with equal parts condensed milk and pour over your tropical fruit salad.

The slow train to a lychee spritz

**MAKES 1 COCKTAIL
OR PUNCH FOR 4
(SEE *NOTE*)**

75 ml (2½ fl oz) dry white
   wine (see *Notes*)
15 ml (½ fl oz) sloe gin
15 ml (½ fl oz) Lychee
   vinegar (opposite)
30 ml (1 fl oz) soda water
   (club soda)
ice cubes, to serve
dash of Orange bitters
   (page 42)
mint sprigs, to garnish

Spritzes have been around for a while but, of late, that simple
mix of wine, bitter and bubble has really taken hold. This particular
cocktail also scales quite well to a punch for enjoying en masse.

Add the wine, gin and vinegar to a highball glass or a large serving
jug if making punch (see *Note*). Gently add the soda, followed by
some ice.

Finish with the bitters and garnish with mint.

Riesling is a good wine to use in this cocktail.

*To make this a punch to serve four, use 450 ml (15 fl oz) of wine,
90 ml (3 fl oz) each of gin and Lychee vinegar, 150 ml (5 fl oz) of
soda water and five dashes of Orange bitters.*

Zeb's cocktail

15 ml (½ fl oz) Lychee
   vinegar (opposite)
90 ml (3 fl oz) Coconut
   water (page 82)
15 ml (½ fl oz) Kaffir lime
   leaf syrup (page 217)
30 ml (1 fl oz) soda water
   (club soda)
ice cubes, to serve
dash of anise liqueur
pineapple sage or regular
   sage, to garnish

I worked with Zeb at Gin Palace, and he had the same love of fresh
lychees that I had (he too carried them in his top pocket). He also
had a fondness for coconut water and, at the time, I didn't really
appreciate it. He kept bringing me different brands until I finally
came around. This one's for you, Zeb. All our favourite things in
one glass.

Add the vinegar, coconut water and syrup to a highball glass.
Stir to combine, then add the soda and gently top with ice.

Finish by floating the liqueur on top. Garnish with pineapple sage.

Mango

Growing up, mangoes weren't something that we had in the fruit bowl, so I assumed they were an expensive fruit – a luxury. So when I did come across them, I gorged myself and wished my parents had more money to buy more mangoes for me. The truth is, mangoes are one of the most widely eaten fruits in the world. It is the national fruit of India, along with Pakistan and the Philippines, and is the national tree of Bangladesh. I guess I just missed out as a kid because my parents didn't like mangoes! The king of mangoes, the Alphonso, is one variety to look out for, reputably living up to the name. I have never had the pleasure of trying one myself as most of them are grown in India and, alas, I've never visited. My favourite variety is the Kensington Pride, which is grown here in Australia and has that perfect balance of honeyed floral sweetness with a touch of acidic freshness.

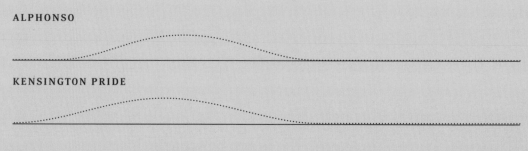

ALPHONSO

KENSINGTON PRIDE

SPRING　　　　　　SUMMER　　　　　　AUTUMN　　　　　　WINTER

Mango vermouth

**MAKES 700 ML
(23½ FL OZ)**

1 mango
750 ml (25½ fl oz/3 cups)
  dry vermouth

I wrote this recipe for my first book, *The Book of Vermouth* (no prizes for guessing the topic), and thought it was such a good prep recipe that I would steal it for this book. It has so many applications and can be used as a substitute for dry vermouth in any classic cocktail that would benefit from a tropical edge. Mango skins are key to this recipe; that's where all the aroma is, and we want to bring that to the vermouth. You'll need to start this recipe the night before you want to enjoy it.

Peel the mango skin with a knife, leaving as much flesh on the stone as possible. Trim the ends of the mango skin to flatten. Add the skins and ends to an airtight container.

Next, cut the mango flesh. Place the mango horizontally on a chopping board and, with a knife, start in the middle and run the knife down the side of the stone, removing as much flesh as possible. Rotate 90 degrees and do the same for the sides. Scrape the remaining mango off the stone with your teeth and enjoy – it's the only way to eat it. Discard the stone in your compost.

Cut the mango flesh into 2 cm (¾ in) slices and add to the container with the skins. Pour in the vermouth, seal and leave to sit overnight in the fridge. The next morning, strain the vermouth and transfer to a sterilised glass bottle (see page 15). Add the skins to the compost and dehydrate the mango flesh (see page 14). The vermouth will last for up to 3 months in the fridge.

For another day

Ginger beer. Add a splash to your ginger beer – the more the better in my opinion.

Steamed fish. Instead of steaming fish in a parcel with white wine, use a 1:1 ratio of mango vermouth to water.

Martini. Make your martini a mango martini.

54 mangoes

Five prime ministers, ten years

45 ml (1½ fl oz) Mango
  vermouth (page 115)
15 ml (½ fl oz) Orange
  sherbet (page 22)
10 ml (¼ fl oz) Citric
  solution (page 216)
5 ml (⅛ fl oz) golden syrup
5 ml (⅛ fl oz) grenadine
  (page 219)
ice cubes, for stirring
dehydrated mango (see
  page 14), to garnish

This cocktail is inspired by the classic El Presidente cocktail (rum, dry vermouth, curaçao and grenadine), which was reportedly named after Mario García Menocal, the president of Cuba from 1913 to 1921, around the time the cocktail showed up. I couldn't decide which recent Australian leader to name this after as a twist on the classic, as we have had five in the past ten years, so I decided to name it after all of them!

Combine all the ingredients in a mixing glass. Stir to combine, then top with ice and stir to chill and dilute.

Strain into a cocktail glass, then garnish with dehydrated mango.

54 mangoes

45 ml (1½ fl oz) Mango
  vermouth (page 115)
45 ml (1½ fl oz) kombucha
15 ml (½ fl oz) Lemongrass
  syrup (page 217)
5 ml (⅛ fl oz) ginger juice
2 drops of natural blue
  food colouring
ice cubes, to serve
dehydrated mango (see
  page 14), to garnish

Kombucha is fermented tea, so one could say that it is funky tea. Since this cocktail contains mangoes, 'funky mangoes' would have sufficed for a name, but that doesn't sound inviting, does it? Something funky that has always appealed, to me at least, is Studio 54, and this funky cocktail pays homage to that nightclub.

Combine all the ingredients in a highball glass and stir to combine.

Top with ice, garnish with mango and funk the night away.

Pome fruits

For me, there is nothing more autumnal than the flavours of pome fruits, which are fruits that have a 'core' of seeds, such as apples and pears. While writing this chapter, I looked back on all the cocktails I developed during my stint at Gin Palace. We changed the cocktail list every season and, flicking through the autumn cocktails, it was all apples, pears and quinces! These items not only make their way into drinks, but onto dinner tables in the form of apple pie, poached pears and quince tarts. All of these dishes and drinks somehow say it's getting colder outside, but it ain't freezing just yet. A couple of other pome fruits that we couldn't squeeze in here are loquats and medlars, which, to be fair, I don't know much about (but I am keen to learn more – perhaps for the next book).

—Shaun

Apple

Apples generally belong in one of two camps: pitters or eaters. 'Eaters' or 'eating' apples do what they say on the tin: they are for eating, and they are delicious. 'Spitters' or 'cider' apples, on the other hand, aren't too tasty in their raw form; as soon as you take a bite you'll want to spit it out. Most of us are familiar with the eating kind, but unless you are big into your cider you probably won't be too familiar with the other.

Cider apples are great for pressing and fermenting into cider. Personally, I have never worked with cider apples, but I have put one in my mouth (and didn't spit it out but only due to sheer will) and I think it is important to note them in these pages.

In Australia, most of the cider I know is made from eating apples, but the ones I've had with cider apples are, in my opinion, superior. Within the eating category, there is a huge number of varieties, from tart Granny Smiths to fujis with their delicate honey flavours, to Braeburns (my favourite), which have a subtle, spicy quality perfect for an apple pie.

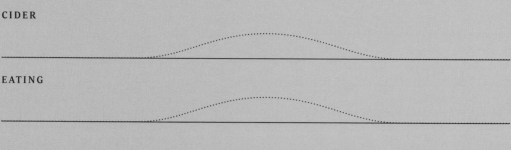

CIDER

EATING

SPRING   SUMMER   AUTUMN   WINTER

Apple-brandy liqueur

**MAKES APPROX. 600 ML
(20½ FL OZ)**

2 g (⅛ oz) ascorbic acid
12 apples
500 ml (17 fl oz/2 cups)
 brandy

Apple juice has a tendency to brown quickly. Behind the bar, I used to squeeze in lime (when in season) with my apple juice to help prevent this. Then I discovered Dave Arnold's book *Liquid Intelligence* and learned that there is a much better way. Juice your apples directly into an ascorbic acid solution. Ascorbic acid, or vitamin C, prevents the apples from browning. It also has a lovely tartness.

For this recipe, we also need to discuss apple molasses. It's made very simply by reducing freshly pressed, sieved apple juice. You have to reduce it a lot – to about 10 per cent of its original volume. Apple molasses, or boiled cider, has been made for centuries. It was a great way to get that appley goodness throughout the year and, in the olden days, it used to be cheaper than sugar, so was frequently used as a sweetener. You'll need to start this recipe the night before.

Dissolve the ascorbic acid in 1 tablespoon water and pour into a container. Juice the apples and pass the juice through a fine-mesh sieve into the ascorbic solution; this should yield about 1 litre (34 fl oz/4 cups). Add the pulp to the brandy and refrigerate overnight.

Pour the apple solution into a saucepan and bring to the boil over a medium heat. Reduce to about 10 per cent of the original volume, i.e. from 1 litre (34 fl oz/4 cups) to 100 ml (3½ fl oz). Remove from the heat and leave to cool overnight.

After a well-deserved night of rest, strain the brandy through a fine-mesh sieve and discard the pulp. Combine the brandy and apple molasses, then pour into a sterilised glass bottle (see page 15). The liqueur will last the winter to keep you warm at night.

For another day

Custard. Spike some custard and serve it with pudding.

Dunking. Sip it neat with some sweet biscuits for dunking.

Spiced milk tea

MAKES 2 CUPS OF TEA

300 ml (10 fl oz)
full-cream (whole) milk
2 green cardamom pods,
crushed
5 g (⅛ oz) diced fresh ginger
5 g (⅛ oz) loose leaf
black tea
5 g (⅛ oz) caster
(superfine) sugar
60 ml (2 fl oz) Apple-
brandy liqueur (page 121)
(optional; see *Note*)
sweet biscuits (cookies),
to serve

I made this recipe and then promptly forgot about it until the tail end of winter when I was doing a bit of 'spring' cleaning. I quickly poured some out and thought to myself, I think it's gotten even better! Being still quite cool at that time of year, I decided to play around with it in a hot drink and, by golly, does it work well with tea. Not so much with the water, though; it was quite diluted. So swapping out the water for milk was easy, then I added a few spices that worked with apples and, hey presto, job done.

Combine all the ingredients except the liqueur and biscuits in a saucepan. Heat gently over a low heat for 5 minutes, then remove from the heat and add the liqueur. Stir for 30 seconds to allow the residual heat of the saucepan to gently warm the liqueur.

Strain into a teapot and serve with dry biscuits.

You can omit this if you are having an alcohol-free day.

Apple rickey

30 ml (1 fl oz) Apple-brandy
liqueur (page 121)
20 ml (¾ fl oz) fresh lime
juice (or verjus, if limes
are not in season; see
page 218)
10 ml (¼ fl oz) Sugar syrup
(page 217)
90 ml (3 fl oz) soda water
(club soda)
ice cubes, to serve
lime twist, to garnish (zest
the lime before juicing
and save the zest)

Rickeys are cocktails made with a spirit mixed with lime, sugar and the bubbliest of water. During my stint at Melbourne's Gin Palace, I certainly made a number of gin rickeys, but also bourbon and even rum (which is a mintless mojito, sort of). Anyway, the lime here really freshens up the liqueur and gives you a much lighter beverage to enjoy.

Combine the liqueur, lime juice and sugar syrup in a highball glass and stir gently. Top with soda water. Gently stir, then top with ice. Gently stir (just kidding). Garnish. Drink gently.

Apple-brandy liqueur

Pear

There is nothing worse than a sandy, gritty pear. I would hate to see the look on my face when I bite into one. That said, pears aren't all bad – quite the contrary. They're great in perry (pear cider), lovely to poach and delightful in tea. At the start of the season, the rich beurre bosc pears are the go-to: nice and soft with hints of warm Christmas spice. Williams is also a good early variety, and I find these a little more buttery. Towards the end of the season, my favourites come out: the corellas. They are tarter and crisper than the aforementioned varieties, they're great eating fruit and wonderful with cheese. If that wasn't enough, the variety is actually an Australian variety, named after a parrot!

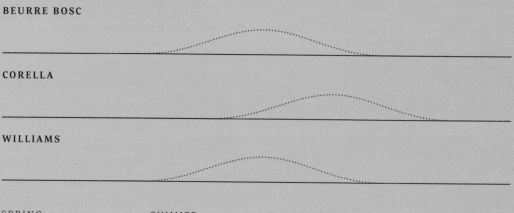

BEURRE BOSC

CORELLA

WILLIAMS

SPRING   SUMMER   AUTUMN   WINTER

Pear tisane ⬙

**MAKES 20 BAGS
OF TISANE**

5 pears
10 g (¼ oz) dried
 chamomile flowers
10 g (¼ oz) dried lemon
 balm
10 g (¼ oz) juniper berries
20 home-made tea bags
 (see page 16)

Many years ago when my girlfriend (now wife) moved in with me, she stocked our cupboards with tea. I wasn't much of a tea drinker back then, but the one she used to drink most often was pear and jasmine, which was quite pleasant. When sitting down to write this book, I thought it would be nice to try to create a tea based around the pear. The recipe is straightforward, but be sure to dehydrate the pears all the way through. It is important to leave the mixture to sit for a week so that the flavours and aromas can homogenise. If you can wait two weeks, then even better.

Core and cut the pears into 1.5 cm (½ in) cubes. Dehydrate in a food dehydrator overnight or in the oven at a low temperature (see page 14).

Combine all the ingredients in an airtight container and let sit for 1 week. You can either portion it out into tea bags or just keep it in the container. It will keep sealed at room temperature for up to 3 months.

For another day

Amp up the flavour. Drop a couple of pear tea bags into the saucepan next time you're poaching pears for a dessert.

Gin. Drop a bag or two into a bottle of gin overnight for your next G&T. Just remove the tea bags the next day.

Poaching fish. Prepare your poaching water with one tea bag per 500 ml (17 fl oz/2 cups) boiling water and leave to infuse for 5 minutes before poaching the fish.

Pear tisane

Long-lunch cup

Diamonds in your wine

**MAKES 1 JUG FOR
4 THIRSTY MOUTHS**

50 ml (1¾ fl oz) gin
300 ml (10 fl oz) riesling
  (off-dry works best here)
300 ml (10 fl oz) sparkling
  apple juice
300 ml (10 fl oz) dry tonic
  water
ice cubes, to serve
fresh pear slices, to
  garnish (see *Note*)
4 Pear tisane tea bags
  (page 125), to serve

When I went ring shopping before I proposed to my wife, I knew nothing of diamonds and their sizes, shapes or carats. When I was getting the run-down of the cuts, I liked the sound of pear – after all, I do have a fondness for food and this was the only food-shaped diamond. It also reminded me of the tea my wife used to drink. Fast forward to today: the cocktail itself is a spritz of a kind, quite refreshing, designed to be served in a large vessel and shared with friends. If you so choose, feel free to garnish each drink with a pear-cut diamond ring …

Combine the gin and riesling in a jug. Gently top with the sparkling apple juice and tonic, then finish with ice.

Garnish with pear slices, then serve alongside four empty glasses with a Pear tisane tea bag in each one.

If pears are not in season, a sprig of mint will suffice.

Long-lunch cup 💧

1 Pear tisane tea bag
  (page 125)
30 ml (1 fl oz) Elderflower
  syrup (page 217)
120 ml (4 fl oz) soda water
  (club soda)
2 cucumber ribbons
ice cubes, to serve

A long lunch doesn't always need to be boozy. A drink such as this is something you could consume all the way through, refreshing the palate between courses, or at the very least spacing out the glasses of wine. Try our Elderflower syrup (page 217) in this recipe, or feel free to buy it if you have a good supplier.

Combine the tea bag and syrup in a glass, finishing with the soda water and cucumber ribbons. Top with ice. *Fin.*

Nashi (Asian pear)

I have always called them nashis and, growing up, mum told me that they were a cross between an apple and a pear. As an adult, I now know that to be false, but it appeared my mum wasn't the only mum telling their kids this; when I was doing research for this book, a few friends mentioned the same thing. There are only two varieties of nashi that I am familiar with, Hosui and Shinko, although many exist. I can't detect a huge difference in taste between the two. The Shinko is a little larger and a little less intense, but they are both sweet, juicy and crisp.

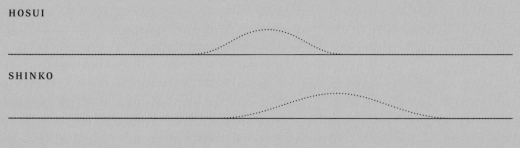

HOSUI

SHINKO

SPRING   SUMMER   AUTUMN   WINTER

Nashishu

**MAKES APPROX. 800 ML
(27 FL OZ) OF SHU-EY
GOODNESS**

5 nashi pears
700 ml (23½ fl oz) sake
100 g (3½ oz) caster
  (superfine) sugar
10 g (¼ oz) malic acid
  (see *Note*)

Shu in Japanese means 'liquor', with famous examples being yuzushu and umeshu. I do have a soft spot for both of these products, but I try not to indulge too often as they come from so far away and that wouldn't be very sustainable of me. So, when we sat down to discuss recipes for this book, Nick and I developed this one as a local *shu* substitute and, I must say, it is quite delightful. You'll need to start this recipe three days ahead of time.

Segment the nashis and place them in a container with the sake. Seal, refrigerate for 3 days, then strain the sake and set aside.

Add the nashi fruit, sugar and 50 ml (1¾ fl oz) water to a saucepan set over a medium heat and simmer for 30 minutes. Strain off the cooking liquid, add the malic acid and allow to cool. Compost the nashi fruit.

Combine the nashi syrup and the sake, then transfer to a sterilised glass bottle (see page 15). It will keep for up to 1 month in the fridge.

Malic acid is available from specialist cookery stores, or online.

For another day

Quince paste. Blitz a small amount of Nashishu with quince paste before adding it to your cheese board.

Bitter lemon soda. Nashishu and bitter lemon is the next G&T. Well, maybe ...

Writer's block

45 ml (1½ fl oz) Nashishu
(opposite)
5 ml (⅛ fl oz) yuzu juice
dash of anise liqueur
90 ml (3 fl oz) soda water
(club soda)
ice cubes, to serve

Naming this drink was incredibly difficult. Once the recipe was developed and tested, I sat in front of my computer for at least an hour trying to come up with a name. Nothing came to me, so I went to bed. The next day, same story, nothing came to me, and by this stage I had spent a few hours procrastinating trying to solve the problem. I figured out that I had spent more time trying to figure out a name than it had taken me to develop and test the cocktail. So I named it writer's block.

Build all the ingredients except the soda water in a highball glass. Gently top with soda water and finish with some ice.

Japanese tiki-style drink

45 ml (1½ fl oz) Nashishu
(opposite)
30 ml (1 fl oz) pineapple
juice
30 ml (1 fl oz) orange juice
10 ml (¼ fl oz) Orgeat
(page 195)
5 ml (⅛ fl oz) Rosemary
honey (page 177)
5 ml (⅛ fl oz) Citric
solution (page 216)
ice cubes, for shaking
crushed ice, to serve
flamed rosemary, to
garnish

The name of this cocktail says it all, really – a tropical combination of ingredients set to confuse and wow your palate. A lot of tiki drinks call for rum, but this one calls for what rum is made of: molasses, along with the usual citrus suspects and a little orgeat for good measure.

Combine all the ingredients in a shaker with ice. Put on your loudest shirt and shake vigorously – the drink, that is.

Strain into a collins glass over crushed ice, then garnish with flamed rosemary. Close your eyes and pretend you're on the beach.

Quince

Most quinces need some kind of cooking to reach their full potential. Apparently there are a couple of varieties that you can attack raw, but I am not familiar with them. Quinces are quite floral, wonderfully aromatic and high in pectin, which means a little can be thrown into your jams or jellies made of other fruits to help them set and give an extra layer of flavour. Champion quinces are good for earlier in the season, but I always hang out for the pineapple quinces, which come a little later. As you would suspect, there is a hint of pineapple in the aroma and, when cooked, they produce a great funky aroma that I really enjoy.

CHAMPION

PINEAPPLE

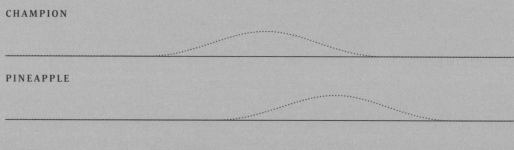

Quince jelly (grandma's recipe)

**MAKES APPROX. 500 G
(1 LB 2 OZ)**

5 quinces
caster (superfine) sugar

There is a story that marmalade was originally made with quinces, as the word marmalade is derived, via a few different languages, from the Portuguese word for quince: *marmelo*. It would be a good guess to assume that, back then, marmalade made from quince would be more expensive to make than marmalade from citrus, in particular bitter orange. And so, marmalade evolved; however, the true marmalade still exists today, made with quinces and served on many a cheese plate under the guise of quince paste or quince jelly. This recipe is from Nick's grandma and, although I haven't had the pleasure of tasting the recipe made by her own hand, I can certainly vouch for the one we have replicated here.

Rub the quinces with a cloth to remove any fluff. Place in a large saucepan and cover with cold water. Bring to the boil, then simmer, uncovered, until very soft. The water will reduce considerably.

Strain the water through a piece of muslin (cheesecloth), squeezing out every last bit of juice, then compost the pulp. Weigh the quince juice and mix with the same weight of sugar in a saucepan. Place over a medium heat and bring to the boil, stirring as you go (only stir until the sugar has dissolved). Continue to boil until the jelly reaches setting point. To test this, place a small saucer in the freezer. Once cold, dollop a bit of jam onto the saucer, wait a few moments, then run your finger through it. If it leaves a clean line with no jelly running into the middle, it is ready. The jelly will keep for up to 1 year in the fridge once opened.

For another day

Cheese. There is a reason you see quince served a lot on cheese boards.

Tea. Use for sweetening your hot tea. I would lean towards black.

For Andy

Before 7 am 💧

2 spoons Quince jelly
  (page 133)
3 spoons natural yoghurt
1 spoon Rosemary honey
  (page 177)
6 spoons Coconut water
  (page 82)

What a way to start the day. A breakfast smoothie of sorts with enough electrolytes to replenish the body from the night before. Use either teaspoons or tablespoons for the measurements to make your smoothie as big or small as you want.

Combine all the ingredients and blitz in a blender or food processor. Break your fast.

For Andy

2 tablespoons Quince jelly
  (page 133)
15 ml (½ fl oz) orange
  curaçao
15 ml (½ fl oz) quinquina
10 ml (¼ fl oz) lemon juice
  (see *Note*)
ice cubes, for shaking and
  serving
90 ml (3 fl oz) tonic water
thyme sprig, to garnish

Andy, a good friend of mine, asked me one year for some Maidenii quinquina to make his yearly batch of quince paste. In return, he would give me some of the finished product. I tell you what, it was incredible. Not your traditional quince paste; it was quite runny, which made it great for using in drinks. This is one of the drinks I made with it and named in his honour.

Combine all the ingredients except the tonic water in a shaker with ice. Shake, then strain into a highball glass. As always, gently top with your tonic, then finish with some ice. Garnish with thyme and toast to Andy.

If lemons aren't in season, substitute with verjus (see page 218).

Vegetables

When it comes to drinks, we don't usually consider using vegetables, (unless it's tomato). However, with the huge variety of vegetables on offer in an array of flavours, colours, shapes and sizes, this seems silly. In cocktails, vegetables can create a great point of difference, and they're also often considerably more accessible and less expensive than fruit. What is required is a little forethought and planning as extraction is, on the whole, a slightly longer process.

Here, we are only just scraping the surface of the vegetables we have access to, focusing on vegetables (and some items that technically aren't vegetables) that have classically been used for drink-making and garnishes. Really, there deserves to be a whole book just based on the subject of drinking your vegetables.

—Nick

Rhubarb

A perennial plant with a peak season over the winter months, rhubarb, for me, has always taken the form of stewed stems with apples for a family pie filling, or been mixed with yoghurt and cereal for breakfast.

One of the biggest misconceptions people have is the association of red stalks and sweetness. In fact, while the bright red stalks are aesthetically appealing, the light pink and green are often the sweetest. And while there aren't often varieties on labels when buying bunches of rhubarb, the colour and width of the stems will give you an indication of what they are. Long, thin, pink stems will most likely be a variety named sunrise. I find this one is the sweetest. The ones that start red at the base and work up to green at the top are most likely Victoria. These are the tartest. And then those with the thick, continuously red stems will be any number of varieties that fit into the red grouping. These have a moderate sweetness and moderate tartness, but look stunning. It is important to note that you should always remove the leaves when preparing rhubarb; they are, in fact, poisonous.

RED

SUNRISE

VICTORIA

SPRING   SUMMER   AUTUMN   WINTER

Rhubarb wine & sour rhubarb purée ⬦

**MAKES 500 ML
(17 FL OZ/2 CUPS)**

RHUBARB WINE
bunch of rhubarb, hops
   and base removed, cut
   into 2 cm (¾ in) lengths
150 g (5½ oz) caster
   (superfine) sugar
50 ml (1¾ fl oz) lemon
   juice (or whey; see *Note*)

RHUBARB PURÉE
300 g (10½ oz) caster
   (superfine) sugar

Rhubarb wine has its origins in the English countryside. I fell in love with the recipe and flavour after watching early River Cottage episodes with a group of English mates. Hugh Fearnley-Whittingstall championed all things being grown and raised around him. This recipe is adapted from those ideas. You will need to start this recipe four days ahead of time.

For the wine, add the rhubarb to a sterilised container (see page 15). Combine the sugar and lemon juice with 1.5 litres (51 fl oz/6 cups) water in a jug and stir to dissolve. Pour the liquid over the rhubarb, then cover the container with muslin (cheesecloth) and leave to sit in a warm, dry spot for 3 days.

Strain the liquid, reserving the rhubarb, and refrigerate to stop the fermentation process. Store for up to 2 weeks.

To make the purée, add the reserved rhubarb pieces to a saucepan with the sugar and 250 ml (8½ fl oz/1 cup) water. Simmer for 45 minutes, then remove from the heat and leave to cool.

Once cool, purée the mixture using a hand-held blender. Refrigerate in an airtight container for up to 1 week or freeze for up to 2 months.

You can make whey by adding citric acid at 10 g (¼ oz) per 1 litre (34 fl oz/4 cups) milk. Combine, then pour into a piece of muslin (cheesecloth) suspended over a bowl. Leave to drain. The whey will be captured in the bowl, leaving behind the curds in the muslin.

For another day

Rhubarb spritz. Combine two parts rhubarb wine, one part dry vermouth and one part soda water (club soda).

Purée through yoghurt. Or soak with water and muesli to make tomorrow's bircher muesli.

Punch. Use the wine in punches, or serve by itself for an afternoon refresher.

Pink gin

60 ml (2 fl oz) Rhubarb
  wine (opposite)
20 ml (¾ fl oz) gin
60 ml (2 fl oz) tonic water
ice cubes, to serve
mint sprig, to garnish

For me, this is a blend of the things that I find most quintessentially English: beautiful pink rhubarb, plentiful G&Ts and mint, which fill the striped cups full of Pimms on the edge of the River Thames at the Henley Royal Regatta. Pink gin traditionally refers to the addition of aromatic bitters to chilled gin. This cocktail toys with the same idea.

Combine the rhubarb wine and gin in a tall glass. Top with tonic, then fill the glass with ice and garnish with a mint sprig.

King of the crop

45 ml (1½ fl oz) fresh apple
  juice
45 ml (1½ fl oz) Iced
  cascara tisane (page 215)
30 ml (1 fl oz) Rhubarb
  purée (opposite)
a few drops of balsamic
  vinegar
apple fan, to garnish
aromatic bitters, to
  garnish (optional)

Rhubarb can be grown from both seeds or from the crown, the crown being the large woody root piece. This terminology has led us to the name of this drink. It will taste just like the apple pies that were at the school fête cake stall, when you would run around with a crown on your head playing dress-ups.

Combine all the cocktail ingredients in a shaker with ice. Shake hard and fast, then strain into a cocktail glass.

To make your apple fan, cut a cheek off an apple, then cut off thin slices. Hold five slices together at one end and secure them with a toothpick, then slowly fan them out at the other end. I like to finish a fan with a dash of aromatic bitters over the top, just for a little extra spice on the nose. Use the fan to garnish your drink.

Pumpkin

Pumpkin, in Australia, refers to all forms of winter squash. They differ from the rest of the squash family in that they are not harvested until they are mature and have developed their hard external skin. Blue pumpkins are the large, pale blue-skinned monsters of the pumpkin family, often weighing around 5 kg (11 lb) each. These are the best roasting pumpkins. The kabocha, or Japanese, pumpkin has very sweet flesh, and is easily the most user-friendly, as cutting through it is far less of a chore than cutting through the larger blue ones. Butternuts are the variety that look like a bell, with a pale orange interior that is nutty, and my favourite for a rich pumpkin soup.

As long as they're stored in a cool, airy environment, pumpkins will last for a number of months, meaning that they will still be around past winter. My mum has converted an old drying rack in the laundry into a resting port for her pumpkins. Interestingly, a pumpkin can take up to three months post-harvest to reach peak ripeness as the vegetable's starches are converted into sugars.

BLUE

BUTTERNUT

KABOCHA

SPRING   SUMMER   AUTUMN   WINTER

Roasted pumpkin syrup

**MAKES APPROX. 500 ML
(17 FL OZ/2 CUPS)**

600 g (1 lb 5 oz) pumpkin
(winter squash), skin and
seeds removed, cut into
4 cm (1½ in) cubes
100 g (3½ oz) brown sugar
200 g (7 oz) caster
(superfine) sugar
1 cinnamon stick

Growing up, I was always confused by the crossover between sweet and savoury flavours. I didn't understand the idea of a savoury pumpkin (winter squash) scone (biscuit), and certainly couldn't comprehend the idea of a pumpkin pie. That was until I lived in Canada and got to experience my first Thanksgiving meal. We were treated to a pumpkin pie and, in a moment, I understood it all. This is, quite simply, a syrup that recreates the flavours of that pie.

Preheat the oven to 180°C (350°F) and roast the pumpkin for 45 minutes.

Make a sugar syrup by combining the sugars with 650 ml (22 fl oz) water in a saucepan and stirring over a medium heat until dissolved, about 5 minutes.

Once the pumpkin is roasted, transfer to a food processor or high-speed blender and blitz to a smooth purée. Pour into another saucepan, add the sugar syrup and cinnamon stick, mix well and simmer over a medium heat for 15 minutes.

Strain the syrup and transfer to a sterilised glass bottle (see page 15). Store in the fridge for up to 2 weeks.

For another day

Roasted pumpkin seeds (pepitas). Mix with tamari for a delicious snack.

Pre-nap tipple. Combine with chai mix for a warm, soothing drink.

Savoury scones. Whip with cream for a great topping for savoury scones (biscuits).

Dark & stormy. Use it to spice up your cocktail.

Trick or treat?

30 ml (1 fl oz) rye whiskey
60 ml (2 fl oz) Pumpkin
  syrup (page 143)
60 ml (2 fl oz) cream soda
ice cubes, to serve

When we were writing this part of the book, it just so happened to be Halloween. Coincidentally, all the ingredients in the cocktail are classically American flavours, hence the name. Spicy, warming and a heap of fun.

Combine the whiskey and pumpkin syrup in a tall glass, giving it a good stir. Add the cream soda, then top with ice and serve with a metal straw.

Must be mad

40 ml (1¼ fl oz) Pumpkin
  syrup (page 143)
40 ml (1¼ fl oz) pineapple
  juice
10 ml (¼ fl oz) apple–cider
  vinegar
10 ml (¼ fl oz) Rosemary
  honey (page 177)
ice cubes, for shaking
rosemary sprig, to garnish

When I suggested this combination of flavours, Shaun promptly told me I must be mad. He was right and wrong at the same time. Think of it like the first time you had fresh fruit in a salad – it's confusing, but it works. And it's delicious.

Combine all the ingredients in a shaker with ice. Give it a strong shake (you want the pineapple juice to really fluff up).

Strain into a cocktail glass and garnish with a sprig of rosemary.

Fennel

Fennel plants can be broken into two types: bulb and herb fennel. The herb variety yields large tops of leafy fronds that are used as a herb. They are perfect for cooking and using to garnish salads. There are a number of varieties, including those with bronze and reddish fronds. The bulb varieties are much more commonly accessible in market stalls and are generally sold by size rather than variety.

When the fennel plant flowers just before winter, you will see roads lined with their beautiful yellow flowers. These flowers can be dried to give you a year's supply of fennel pollen.

Fennel seeds will come next, after the flowers die away. The heads of the stems are dried out in order to release the seeds, and they are popular in Mediterranean dishes.

BULB

HERB

SPRING   SUMMER   AUTUMN   WINTER

Roasted fennel anglaise

**MAKES APPROX.
2 LITRES (68 FL OZ/
8 CUPS)**

2 fennel bulbs, quartered
500 ml (17 fl oz/2 cups)
   full-cream (whole) milk
2 tablespoons fennel
   seeds
1 litre (34 fl oz/4 cups)
   thickened (whipping)
   cream
2 teaspoons salt
6 egg yolks (see *Note*)
460 g (1 lb/2 cups) caster
   (superfine) sugar

For another day

Dessert. Warm the
custard and serve it with
Rhubarb purée (page 140).

Ice cream. Churn it into
a dessert to blow your
friends' minds.

Frappé. Shake with anise
liqueur for an incredible
frappé.

This is a recipe that I made for a cocktail competition in early 2018.
I presented it at the Diageo World Class Australian finals. The idea
of the competition was to work directly with primary producers.
This drink aims to showcase the difference in flavours between the
seeds and the bulbs. The fennel in the anglaise has a very medicinal,
soothing anise edge. The only problem is that it is a little bit
moreish. After making a batch to test cocktail specs, it disappeared
from the fridge very quickly, meaning I had to whip up a second
batch for the competition itself. I blamed my housemates, but I
might have also had some for a midnight snack after work one night.
You will need to start this recipe one day in advance.

Preheat the oven to 180°C (350°F).

Roast the fennel for 45 minutes, then soak the roasted fennel
in the milk for 24 hours in the fridge.

Meanwhile, dry-roast the fennel seeds in a saucepan for
5 minutes, then soak them in the cream for 24 hours in the fridge.
Strain both the cream and the milk. Compost the fennel and seeds.

Combine the milk, cream and salt in a saucepan over a medium
heat, stirring until it hits 85°C (185°F) on a cooking thermometer.
At the same time, whisk the egg yolks and sugar together in a
bowl until combined.

Add half of the milk mixture to the egg mixture and stir to
combine, then pour the egg custard into the saucepan with the
remaining milk mixture. Stir slowly over a low heat until it reaches
75°C (167°F). Remove from the heat, then strain into a bowl and
place the bowl in an ice bath to help bring down the temperature
quickly. Refrigerate the anglaise in an airtight container to thicken
up. It will keep for about 2 weeks in the fridge.

*Reserve the egg whites for your next whisky sour (they will keep
in the fridge for about 3 days).*

A little help from our friends

80 ml (2½ fl oz/⅓ cup)
   Roasted fennel anglaise
   (opposite)
20 ml (¾ fl oz) dark rum
20 ml (¾ fl oz) apricot
   brandy liqueur
fennel leaf and pollen,
   to garnish

This is a simplified version of the cocktail I made for the competition (see opposite). The name refers to how much farmers and regional producers rely on community and helping hands to get through day-to-day working life while suffering at the hands of Mother Nature. This cocktail is an example of the way different flavours and textures integrate at different temperatures. It's best served at room temperature so that the dairy fats are warm enough to integrate with the alcohol. Serve instead of dessert to round out a long lunch.

Combine all the ingredients except the garnish in a ceramic mug and whisk very gently with either a Japanese matcha whisk or a small kitchen whisk, just enough to integrate all the ingredients. Dust a small pinch of fennel pollen over the top and drape a leaf over the side to finish.

Fennel fluffy duck ⬡

90 ml (3 fl oz) lemonade
   (lemon soda)
30 ml (1 fl oz) Roasted
   fennel anglaise (opposite)
10 ml (¼ fl oz) Oak syrup
   (page 217)
toasted marshmallows,
   to serve

A fluffy duck is a nineties cocktail with advocaat, a Dutch custard liqueur. My favourite version is topped with lemonade, giving it a spider-like consistency (you know, those soft drink and ice cream numbers Shaun was talking about on page 109). This is just that, but with a slightly adult flavour twist.

In a tall glass, add a splash of the lemonade to the anglaise and oak syrup. Give it a really good stir to combine, then top with the rest of the lemonade, allowing a glorious foam to form. To round out the indulgence, serve with toasted marshmallows on the side.

Celery

In Australia, celery is sold all year round, but it reaches its absolute peak of flavour in the winter months. We also don't see celery sold by variety here. In this book, we are referring to green-stalked celery.

When I was growing up, celery was presented as a snack, filled with hummus, peanut butter or cream cheese. I later realised how esteemed this vegetable is. It is an integral component in the holy trinity of a mirepoix with onion and carrot, which forms the base of a large number of classical European dishes.

In regards to cocktails, we best know celery as a garnish sticking out the side of a bloody mary. Or, in the bartending world, as a late-night nibble behind the bar.

CELERY

Acidulated celery juice ⬭

**MAKES APPROX. 500 ML
(17 FL OZ/2 CUPS)**

500 g (1 lb 2 oz) celery
  stalks
15 ml (½ fl oz) apple-cider
  vinegar
10 g (¼ oz) citric acid
pinch of salt

Celery juice has, for a long time, been used solely for morning juice cleanses, but it deserves more. This recipe gives the juice a little more stability, so that it will hold both its colour and flavour for longer than a couple of hours. Just remember to give the juice a good shake when you take it out of the fridge to make sure it is homogonised before you pour it.

Juice the celery in a centrifugal juicer (see page 13), then strain it through a fine-mesh sieve and combine with the remaining ingredients in a sterilised glass bottle (see page 15). Seal with a lid and give it a good shake to combine and dissolve. This will keep in the fridge for 2 days.

For another day

Morning cleanser. Combine with fresh apple juice for a bright, clean drink that's heaps better than kale.

Dress it up. Cut with basil oil and lemon juice for a salad dressing.

Brunch bloody mary. Combine with Passata (page 159) and your choice of spirit for a fragrant bloody mary.

Celery southside

30 ml (1 fl oz) gin
20 ml (¾ fl oz) Mint-stem
  cordial (page 173)
30 ml (1 fl oz) Acidulated
  celery juice (page 151)
ice cubes, for shaking
2 mint sprigs, plus 1 mint
  leaf to garnish

A southside is one of my favourite cocktails; it's ssentially a mojito, but with gin and served in a cocktail glass. This version gets the acid from the celery juice that would regularly come from lime juice. This, combined with the mint, makes for a fantastically fresh pick-me-up. It's a great bloody mary brunch alternative too.

Shake and bake, baby. Combine all the ingredients in a shaker with ice. Shake hard and fast, then strain into a cocktail glass.

This is a cocktail that will need to be fine-strained as well (see page 13). Finish with a mint leaf on top.

Green & dry ◌

60 ml (2 fl oz) Acidulated
  celery juice (page 151)
2 dashes of Orange bitters
  (page 42)
90 ml (3 fl oz) dry ginger ale
ice cubes, to serve
2 tarragon sprigs, to
  garnish
hot sauce, to serve
  (optional)

Absinthe is often referred to as the green fairy. Over the years, the green fairy has attracted a lot of myth and fanfare – a creature embodying artistic liberty and a free lifestyle. The relation here is that absinthe is produced with *artemisia absinthium*, or the common wormwood, of which tarragon (*artemisia dracunculus*) is closely related. This riff is one of our favourite low-alcohol combinations: ginger ale with vegetal celery juice standing in for vermouth.

Combine the juice, orange bitters and ginger ale in a highball glass, stir gently, then add ice and garnish with the tarragon.

Serve with hot sauce on the side, just in case a little extra kick is required.

Green & dry

Celery southside

Cucumber

Another confusing one. It's technically a tropical fruit, but we think of it more as a very juicy vegetable for salads. And they're not just good for a classic cucumber sandwich, either.

Cucumbers come in green, yellow and white and are commonly named after other fruits that they resemble – for example, watermelon, for the ripple of dark and light green on the skin, and apple and lemon, due to both colour and bulbous shapes.

Most commonly, it is the Lebanese (also referred to as Persian) cucumber that you will find. It has green, sweet flesh and is very easy to use. Or the telegraph (long) cucumber, which, as the name suggests, is a long pole of a cucumber.

Another personal favourite cucumber is the crystal variety, in particular the crystal apple. This cucumber looks like a small melon, and is sweet and crispy like its namesake. If you can get your hands on one, your salad game will greatly increase.

CRYSTAL

LEBANESE

TELEGRAPH

SPRING   SUMMER   AUTUMN   WINTER

Cucumber shrub & pickled cucumbers ⬦

MAKES APPROX. 500 ML (17 FL OZ/2 CUPS)

300 ml (10 fl oz)
   apple-cider vinegar
100 g (3½ oz) caster
   (superfine) sugar
5 g (⅛ oz) salt
1 cucumber
5 g (⅛ oz) fresh dill

A shrub is a drinking vinegar, a means of preserving flavour and adding a non citrus based–acid to drinks. The idea for a cucumber shrub originally stemmed from the pickleback shot, a popular American trick of following a whiskey shot with a chaser of pickle brine. The fresh, green and vegetal elements of the cucumber play really well against the vinegar here, making a zesty and invigorating mixer. The added byproduct is the pickled cucumber. Pickled cucumbers are, in my book, a mandatory element for any good sandwich, grazing board and household fridge. You'll need to start this recipe three days ahead of time.

Combine all the ingredients except the cucumber and dill in a saucepan with 100 ml (3½ fl oz) water. Bring to the boil over a medium–high heat, stirring to dissolve the sugar, then remove from the heat.

Dice up the cucumber and add to an airtight container with the dill. Pour the cider mixture over the top. Allow to cool, then seal and refrigerate for 3 days before using.

For another day

Fancy up your G&T. Just add a splash of cucumber shrub.

Fish cure. Combine with salt to cure fish for thirty minutes before lightly searing.

Panzanella. Use the shrub to soak your bread for this classic Italian salad.

Antipasti. Serve the pickled cucumbers on a meat or cheese board, or with crudité.

A day in the sheds

20 ml (¾ fl oz) apple
  brandy (the younger
  the better)
20 ml (¾ fl oz) Cucumber
  shrub (page 155)
10 ml (¼ fl oz) sweet
  fortified wine
rock ice, to serve
thyme salt, to garnish
potato chips and pickled
  cucumbers, to serve

During the winter months, as we make the trek up to the apple sheds in Harcourt to clean up after vermouth vintage, it gets a little cold. Shaun is known to have a bottle of brandy on hand, just to help warm up. When we're up there, sustenance is also required: more often than not in the form of a loaf of bread, some meat and cheeses, and always some pickles. This is a coming together of all those things from those cold winter days.

Combine all the ingredients in a glass over a large piece of rock ice and garnish with some thyme salt.

To be honest, we rarely make just one of these; they're best shared with friends and served with pickled cucumbers and some salty potato chips.

Shrub a dub dub

30 ml (1 fl oz) Cucumber
  shrub (page 155)
wasabi, to taste
3 fresh coriander (cilantro)
  sprigs
ice cubes, for shaking and
  serving
60 ml (2 fl oz) dry ginger ale
slice of capsicum (bell
  pepper), to garnish

I worked on this drink with Shaun, who worked with a gentleman by the name of James Whittington, who has since passed away. His nickname was Dub and the story goes that the last drink he served was inside a capsicum (bell pepper). He also had a penchant for wasabi packets (actually, horseradish) and pickles. I never had the pleasure of meeting him, but his legacy lives on in those he worked with. This is for him.

Combine the cucumber shrub, wasabi and coriander in a shaker with ice. Shake well, then strain into a glass.

Top with dry ginger ale and ice, then garnish with a slice of capsicum.

Tomato

Technically a fruit, tomatoes are the highlight of summer for me. Nothing says summer is here more than a juicy BLT (bacon, lettuce and tomato) sandwich, with big, ugly, sweet tomatoes.

My absolute favourite tomato is the beefsteak. It looks almost prehistoric, with ravines running down the side. Its flavour is immense.

In the seasonality chart, we have chosen to group the regular round tomatoes as one category. These are the most accessible, made up of a number of varieties that enable a longer season. The cherry tomato in its different forms will also fall into this category.

Green zebra tomatoes are sharp and acidic, perfect for making chutney or a personal guilty pleasure of a bar snack: fried greens. Roma tomatoes are the oval-shaped ones most commonly used in dehydrating or sun-drying, but they are also used to make passata, as they have a little more structure.

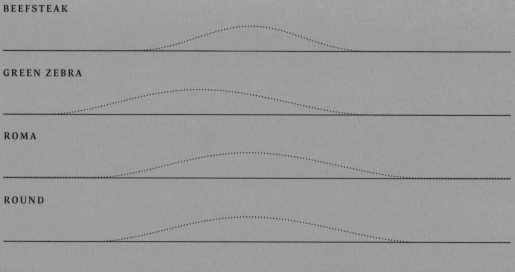

BEEFSTEAK

GREEN ZEBRA

ROMA

ROUND

SPRING   SUMMER   AUTUMN   WINTER

Passata ⬦

**MAKES APPROX. 800 ML
(27 FL OZ)**

**1.5 kg (3 lb 5 oz) tomatoes
  (see _Notes_)
10 g (¼ oz) bird's eye chilli
20 g (¾ oz) sea salt**

Passata is, essentially, just tomatoes that have been cooked down to liquid form. Every summer at Gin Palace, we would make large batches and bottle it up into individual portions, forty or fifty serves at a time.

Personally, I much prefer passata-making as a family activity – a point in summer when you get everyone together to form a production line and churn out a year's supply of future pasta sauces.

Combine all the ingredients in a saucepan and blitz with a hand-held blender until smoothish. Bring to the boil, then simmer for 1 hour.

Strain through a chinoise, pushing as much pulp through as you can. Transfer to a sterilised glass bottle (see page 15).

Ask for second-grade tomatoes, which usually come with a few blemishes but are often riper.

If making larger quantities, sterilise bottles and fill them while the passata is hot. Seal and put aside to last the year.

For another day

Spanish tomato bread. Use tomato passata for a cheat's way to make it. Just add olive oil and salt. Maybe some cured pork.

Bloody mary. Use for all your bloody mary needs. It works especially well with vermouth.

Fetil & bazza

45 ml (1½ fl oz) Passata
(page 159)
20 ml (¾ fl oz) sweet
vermouth
10 ml (¼ fl oz) peated
whisky
1 teaspoon dukkah
feta, to garnish
a basil leaf, to garnish

Shaun and I were working through names for drinks – not a strong point for either of us. As usual, we got sidetracked and instead discussed the accoutrement that may be served as a drink's garnish. In the excitement of a lightbulb moment, Shaun blurted out, 'fetil and bazza'. I didn't understand. What he meant was feta and basil. We had both the name and the garnish sorted right then!

Combine all the ingredients except the garnishes in a shaker. Shake short and fast, then dump all the contents into a tall glass (don't strain) so that you retain the little textures of dukkah. Balance two cubes of feta and a basil leaf on top.

Season's change cocktail

MAKES 2 COCKTAILS

60 ml (2 fl oz) fennel juice
60 ml (2 fl oz) Passata
(page 159)
40 ml (1¼ fl oz) verjus
(see page 218)
2 teaspoons Rosemary
honey (page 177)
ice cubes, for shaking
rosemary sprig, to garnish

This cocktail celebrates the moment when one season passes into the next. In late autumn, the tomato season is drawing to a close and the baton is passed to the fennel crop, which is just coming into full bloom. A fresh, brunch-time reviver for the time of year, where it is no longer too hot to be in the midday sun but not yet at the point where you need to rug up.

Combine all the ingredients in a shaker with ice. Slowly roll around to combine before dumping the contents into two collins glasses.

Garnish with a flamed rosemary sprig both for aroma and a little bit of theatre.

Herbs

The most sustainable way to get herbs into your drinks is to grow them at home. Luckily, you don't need to have a green thumb to be successful – just a little patience and some sun, soil and water. I have been growing herbs in my backyard for quite a few years now with a decent success rate on the whole, which goes to show how easy they are to manage, because I don't consider myself a very good gardener. The other benefits of gardening, besides the glut of a harvest, are its calming effects and the sense of accomplishment you get from seeing things grow. That's when something in my head says, 'You grew that, you legend!' I'm not sure if gardening affects everyone in this way, but I find it such a therapeutic and peaceful task. To improve my success, I reached out to an expert gardener, a friend of mine named Liam Spurrell from Spurrell Foraging, who has given me some tips on growing herbs that I will share with you throughout this chapter. Thank you for your help, Liam, and to all you reading, happy growing!

—Shaun

Basil

When I first moved out of home, I would buy basil for a specific dish and then either not use it or only use a little before the bulk of it would need to be tossed into the compost. It wasn't until much later that someone made the obvious suggestion that I could freeze whatever was left over. To do this, just blanch the basil in hot water for a couple of seconds, then transfer to an ice bath, dry off and stick it in a bag in the freezer. Genius, right? There are a few interesting varieties of basil out there, sweet being the one I am most familiar with. It's perfect for garnishing any red pasta sauce or other Mediterranean dish. Thai basil is great too: a little heavier on the anise, though. Lemon basil is also good, and has – you guessed it – a lemony tang.

PLANT
Seeds or seedlings in spring

GROW
In full sun and well-drained soil

Water regularly

Companion plant with tomatoes

HARVEST
Pick frequently through spring and autumn for a continuous supply

Pick and dry for winter use

Basil oil ⬡

**MAKES APPROX. 100 ML
(3½ FL OZ)**

**1 bunch of basil
100 ml (3½ fl oz)
  extra-virgin olive oil**

This recipe is a great way to create a liquid form of basil to use in drinks. I treat it like bitters, usually finishing a drink with the oil so that it floats on top, which engages your olfactory senses as you drink. Blanching the basil in hot water and shocking it in cold water is key, as it prevents the basil from tasting muddy. You will need to start this recipe the night before.

Prepare an ice bath.

Snip away the bottom of the basil stems, then dunk the leaves in boiling water. Immediately plunge them into the ice bath. Drain, then transfer the leaves to a blender and blitz with the olive oil. Pour into an airtight container and leave to sit overnight.

Suspend a piece of muslin (cheesecloth) over a bowl and pour in the olive oil, then transfer the oil to a sterilised glass bottle (see page 15). Store for up to 2 months.

For another day

Margarita. Float a few drops on top of your next margarita (or your next margherita pizza!).

Cottage cheese. Just a drizzle on top.

Tomato salad. Cut the oil with a small amount of balsamic and pour over in-season, juicy, ripe tomatoes.

Virgin Mary

Pickled basil #5

8 basil leaves
30 ml (1 fl oz) apple liqueur
5 ml (⅛ fl oz) apple-cider
  vinegar
90 ml (3 fl oz) cucumber
  juice
ice cubes, to serve
basil leaf and Basil oil
  (page 165), to garnish

This particular cocktail has evolved over the past few years as I have adjusted the base ingredients. There has always been fresh basil, some form of vinegar and something sweet. The something sweet here is apple liqueur but, if you can't find a local liqueur, you can use an apple brandy or the apple brandy liqueur on page 121. Just use half apple brandy and half Sugar syrup (page 217). The cucumber juice provides the freshness and ties everything together in a nice little bow.

Add the basil leaves to a highball glass and gently press on them with the back of a spoon. Top with the apple liqueur, apple-cider vinegar and cucumber juice, and then with some ice.

Garnish with a basil leaf and some basil oil.

Virgin Mary ◌

120 ml Passata (page 159)
30 ml (4 fl oz) fresh
  orange juice
15 ml (½ fl oz) verjus
  (see page 218)
pinch of smoked paprika
salt and pepper, to taste
ice cubes, to serve
Basil oil (page 165), to float

The non-alcoholic version of the infamous brunch staple. One of the funniest things I have seen in recent times is the lengths some venues will go to when it comes to garnishing their mary variations. These garnishes have ranged from the usual suspects of celery and cucumber to extravagant fried chicken and sliders. This book simply isn't long enough to list all the 'inspirational' ideas people have come up with over the years, but I encourage you to have a look on the internet (or the opposite page!) for inspiration. This recipe does not contain alcohol, but if you do need a little hair of the dog, 30 ml (1 fl oz) sweet vermouth will do just fine.

Combine all the ingredients except the oil and ice in a highball glass, then season to taste.

Top with ice, stirring to combine and chill. Float as much oil on the top as you like. Go crazy with your garnish and take a selfie with your creation.

Coriander

Coriander (also known as cilantro and Chinese parsley) has always been the most polarising of herbs; it has lovers and haters. Apparently there have been studies that link a genetic variation in DNA to distaste for the herb's pungency. I am certainly not qualified to comment on this. All I know is that I like the stuff. The leaves are great with anything spicy, and I would hazard a guess that the majority of gins produced use the seeds in their 'secret' blends.

PLANT

Seeds or seedlings in spring

GROW

In full sun or semi-shade

Water regularly

Companion plant with carrots, broccoli and rocket (arugula)

Attracts bees

HARVEST

During spring and autumn

45 days to maturity

After flowering, harvest brown seeds then dry them to use in cooking

Verdita ⬙

MAKES APPROX. 900 ML
(30½ FL OZ)

½ ripe pineapple
1 cucumber
3 green chillies
1 bunch of coriander
  (cilantro)
5 g (⅙ oz) salt
pinch of ground black
  pepper
pinch of ground white
  pepper
pinch of coriander seeds

This could be the easiest recipe in this book. Just gather your ingredients, blanch and blitz. It is also a recipe that can be tweaked easily if you want to add or take something away. Both verditas (little green) and sangritas (little blood) are often served as accompaniments to tequila. Nick and I came up with this recipe together based on what we had seen at various bars during our 'research phase' for the book. As mentioned on page 165, blanching and refreshing your herbs is key for locking out any unpalatable muddy flavours.

Prepare an ice bath.

Remove the skins from the pineapple and cucumber and compost them, then blitz all the ingredients in a blender. Pass through a coarse sieve and transfer to a sterilised glass bottle (see page 15). Drink within 1 week.

For another day

Sake. Add one part sake to three parts Verdita.

Agave spirits. Use as originally intended, alongside an agave spirit.

Tacos. Great to serve with tacos.

Beer is what's for breakfast

1 part Verdita (opposite)
1 part Passata (page 159)
1 part beer
hot sauce, to taste
ice cubes, to serve

There is a beverage called a Michelada, which is essentially a beer bloody mary. The choice of beer is pretty important; it should be the most flavourless one you can find. Anything too flavoursome will create too many competing flavours. The same can be said for this cocktail – look for something local, light and simple rather than something that is going to overwhelm the drink. This can easily be made into a pitcher for brunch with friends and, as the recipe is in easy equal parts, there are no excuses for not making enough for everyone!

Choose a vessel to accommodate your thirst. Pour in the Verdita and Passata and stir. Gently top with beer, stirring continuously. Add as much hot sauce as you can handle, then finish with some ice.

2&5 ◌

90 ml (3 fl oz) Verdita
  (opposite)
40 g (1½ oz) celery
20 g (¾ oz) apple
20 g (¾ oz) carrot
20 g (¾ oz) fennel bulb
1 teaspoon honey
ice cubes, to serve

Growing up, we were taught that a healthy diet consisted of 2&5, that being two serves of fruit and five serves of veggies each day. Mum was pretty good when we were kids; we got well-balanced meals but, once I left home, the rules went out the window. I'm not sure if this beverage would meet the daily requirements for a 2&5, but there are certainly two types of fruit in there alongside five veggies.

Combine all the ingredients except the ice in a blender and blitz. Pour into a tall glass. Ice it up and drink away your worries.

Mint

The weed of the garden and probably the most used herb in bars thanks to one cocktail: the mojito. For those of you who aren't aware, a mojito is essentially a daiquiri (rum, lime and sugar) with fresh mint, served over crushed ice. Because of the mojito's popularity, I have picked countless bunches of mint for bar prep over the years; even if it does make your fingers black, it's kind of therapeutic. Well, that's true for me anyway – you couldn't get Nick to prep mint at gunpoint; he hates it!

There are many different varieties of mint out there, but I am most familiar with spearmint, also known as common mint. Peppermint is a little spicier, chocolate mint has a hint of cacao, and then there is pineapple mint, which also does what it says on the tin. Mint is also super easy to grow, but people always warned me that it would take over my garden. My answer was always, so what? More mojitos for everyone.

PLANT
Seeds or plant in spring

GROW
In moist conditions
Vigorous grower
Companion plant with cabbage and tomatoes

HARVEST
Pick frequently during spring and autumn for a continuous supply

Mint-stem cordial

**MAKES APPROX. 500 ML
(17 FL OZ/2 CUPS)**

1 bunch of mint of your
  choice
350 g (12½ oz) caster
  (superfine) sugar
10 g (¼ oz) citric acid

As mentioned, prepping mint can be the bane of some bartenders'
existence (not mine), not to mention that it can be quite wasteful.
There is a lot of aroma in the stem, which is quite often discarded in
favour of the leaves. This recipe uses mainly the wasted parts – the
stems – to make a cordial. You will only need around half the leaves
from the bunch, so reserve the rest for all your mojitoing needs,
or freeze them by blanching the leaves as described on page 165.

Pick the mint leaves. Snip off and compost the black bottoms
of the stems.

Combine the sugar, 350 ml (12 fl oz) water, the citric acid and
mint stems in a saucepan and bring to the boil. Reduce the heat
slightly and simmer for 15 minutes. Drop in half of the mint leaves
for the last 30 seconds of cooking time, then immediately strain.
Transfer to a sterilised glass bottle (see page 15). Store for up to
1 month.

For another day

Peas. Toss your peas with butter and a wee dash of cordial.

Soda. Three parts soda, one part cordial and a bunch of
mint leaves.

Minted ramos

30 ml (1 fl oz) gin
30 ml (1 fl oz) thickened
  (whipping) cream
20 ml (¾ fl oz)
  lemon juice
15 ml (½ fl oz) egg white
  (see *Note*)
10 ml (¼ fl oz) Mint-stem
  cordial (page 173)
dash of orange-blossom
  water
ice cubes, for shaking
60 ml (2 fl oz) soda water
  (club soda)
mint sprig, to garnish

There is a cocktail called a Ramos gin fizz, a delightful gin sour of sorts with orange blossom and cream. When I learned how to make this beverage, I was told you had to shake it for a very long time – seven minutes, I think, was the goal. The idea was to fully emulsify and thicken the cream, making a textural sensation. This cocktail takes inspiration from that classic with just a hint of mint.

Combine all the ingredients except the soda water, mint and ice in a shaker and dry shake. Next, wet shake – add some ice and shake for 7 minutes for purists, 5 minutes to get the job done and 3 minutes for those in a rush. Strain into a collins glass.

Pour the soda water into the shaker with the ice and give it a quick swirl, then top the cocktail with the contents. Garnish with a mint sprig and rest your weary arms.

You'll only need one egg for this, and will have white left over.

Green-tea spider ◌

100 ml (3½ fl oz) Iced
  green tea (page 214)
30 ml (1 fl oz) Mint-stem
  cordial (page 173)
50 ml (1¾ fl oz) lemonade
  (lemon soda)
1 scoop of vanilla ice
  cream
mint sprig, to garnish
  (optional)

Spiders were big when I was growing up: both the eight-legged variety and the beverage. It wasn't until I moved to the UK that I discovered that spiders (the beverage) are an Australian thing, and that they are known elsewhere as ice-cream floats or sodas. Apparently us Australians called this drink a spider because, when the bubbles from the soda hit the ice cream, a wonderful web-like reaction of froth appears in the glass. I like the name spider but, then again, I'm Australian and I'm used to both forms of spiders, be they poisonous or liquid.

Add the tea and cordial to a soda glass. Gently add the lemonade, then plop in the ice cream. If you like, garnish with a mint sprig and serve with a long parfait spoon. Imbibe.

Green-tea spider

Rosemary

Buying rosemary instead of growing it is pretty daft. I can't stress enough how easy this particular herb is to grow. You would have to have an anti-green thumb (a purple thumb, perhaps) to kill it. Another bonus is that it's there all year round, ready to pluck for your next lamb roast or to spice up your G&T. An interesting use I have seen quite a bit of lately is torching the rosemary before using it as a garnish. The scent works quite well with darker spirits and stronger flavours. Anise liqueurs love a little rosemary, and a little fire can give them an extra layer of aroma.

PLANT
Seeds or plant in spring

GROW
Hardy, survives in dry conditions
Easily grown from cuttings
Attracts bees

HARVEST
Pick frequently year round
for a continuous supply

Rosemary honey ◌

MAKES APPROX. 400 G (14 OZ)

400 g (14 oz) strong local honey
7 rosemary sprigs
pinch of sea salt

The aim of this recipe is to create a liquid form of rosemary that can be used in drinks. The type of honey you use does make a difference here. With rosemary being a strong flavour, an equally strong-flavoured honey is your best bet. I am partial to a leatherwood honey, but any strong local honey will be just fine.

Combine all the ingredients in a saucepan with 100 ml (3½ fl oz) water. Bring to a gentle simmer and cook for 10 minutes. Remove from the heat and allow to cool, then strain and pour into a sterilised glass jar (see page 15). Store for up to 6 months.

For another day

Ricotta. On toast with a little honey.

Bees knees. A gin, lemon and honey cocktail.

Pork roast. Glaze your meat with it before roasting.

Boozeless old fashioned

60 ml (2 fl oz) Brunswick
 Aces Hearts Blend or
 local hydrosol of your
 choice (see page 11)
1 teaspoon Rosemary
 honey (page 177)
dash of Orange bitters
 (page 42)
ice cubes, to serve
rosemary sprig, to garnish

The story goes that the word 'cocktail' was first described in print in 1806. It said that a cocktail contained four ingredients: spirit, water, sugar and bitters. In this day and age, the spirit can be any spirit, the water is the ice, bitters are bitters and the sugar can come in various forms: agave, maple syrup, honey and sugarcane to name a few. This drink isn't an old fashioned because there is no spirit, but it best describes the drink. Brunswick Aces is a hydrosol. It is delightful, and there are more and more hydrosols popping up, so look for something local to try in this beverage.

Combine all the ingredients in an old fashioned glass, then stir to combine. Add a small amount of ice and stir to dilute and chill said beverage.

Garnish with rosemary.

Brunch time

90 ml (3 fl oz) Passata
 (page 159)
30 ml (1 fl oz) fortified
 wine (see *Note*)
2 teaspoons Rosemary
 honey (page 177)
5 ml (⅛ fl oz) apple-cider
 vinegar
ice cubes, to serve
burnt rosemary sprig,
 to garnish

When I used to make my own passata (puréed tomatoes), I would put rosemary in it. I'm not sure why I stopped. I suppose it was because you can always add an ingredient, but you can't take it away. Tomato and rosemary are best buds, especially in drinks. But, as the rosemary comes via the honey, this drink will be a little sweet, hence the use of apple-cider vinegar to balance it.

Combine all the ingredients in a highball glass. Give it a stir to combine, then top with ice and stir again to chill.

Garnish with a burnt rosemary sprig and enjoy.

Something sweet and light is ideal, but don't use something that's dry and has been in a barrel for a long time. Go for something local and ruby port–like.

Thyme

I think my favourite thing about thyme is the puns that often go along with it – I don't have thyme to list them all. That aside, it is also quite easy to grow and maintain. There are quite a few varieties of thyme, and one of my favourites – besides common thyme – would be lemon thyme. It works really well in the prep recipe in this chapter, giving just a little citric aroma to lift it to new heights.

PLANT
Seeds or plant in spring

GROW
In full sun
Hardy, survives in dry conditions
Attracts bees

HARVEST
Pick frequently in spring and autumn for a continuous supply
Pick and dry for winter use

Smoked thyme salt

**MAKES APPROX. 200 G
(7 OZ)**

1 bunch of thyme, with
  stems
200 g (7 oz) local
  sea salt flakes
pinch of onion powder
pinch of garlic powder

Salt really is underused in beverages, considering how much of
a difference it can make. A little bit of salt in a cocktail can really
tie flavours together, and this wasn't something I learned until
well into my bartending career. In this recipe, we are flavouring
the salt to give it an extra je ne sais quoi, if you will. The powders
complement and emphasise the intensity of the thyme, so I would
highly recommend using them (but, if dietary requirements forbid
it, then leave them out). You'll need to start this recipe one week
ahead of time.

Take three-quarters of the thyme, put it in a jar and muddle. Take
the remaining one-quarter and lightly torch it for a smokey flavour.
You can do this on the barbecue, with a blowtorch or on a gas
stove; just light the flame and then blow it quickly. Make sure you
are safe and use tongs to hold the thyme.

Combine all the ingredients in a sterilised glass jar (see page 175)
and shake. Seal, then leave to sit for around 1 week, shaking daily.
Pour the salt mix onto a tray and remove the thyme stems, then
store in an airtight container for up to 6 months.

For another day

Crispy chicken skin. Rub salt into the skin before roasting.

Dirty martini. Use in place of the olive brine for you next dirty
martini – a pinch will do.

Bitter liqueurs. If you enjoy a bitter liqueur on the rocks,
try a pinch of thyme salt in your next glass.

Thyme for a smoking gin-ade

90 ml (3 fl oz) fresh
  lemonade (see *Note*)
30 ml (1 fl oz) gin
pinch of Smoked thyme
  salt (page 181)
ice cubes, to serve
thyme sprig, to garnish

I'm soon to be a father for the first time, so I am practising my dad jokes wherever possible.

Fresh lemonade should always be made the old-fashioned way (see *Note*).

Combine all the ingredients in a highball glass. Top with ice and garnish with a thyme sprig. Have a pun-ny day.

Mix four parts lemon juice with two parts water and one part Sugar syrup (page 217). However, if that isn't possible, a good-quality, store-bought lemonade (lemon soda) will suffice.

Honey, do you have thyme for apple juice? ◌

120 ml (4 fl oz) fresh
  apple juice
30 ml (1 fl oz) verjus
  (see page 218)
1 teaspoon Rosemary
  honey (page 177)
pinch of Smoked thyme
  salt (page 181)
ice cubes, to serve
thyme sprig, to garnish
apple slice, to garnish

I'm especially proud of the name for this one; it certainly put a smile on my dial. I think apples work well with thyme, and a quick internet search has confirmed my suspicions. The verjus is a must, as this drink can be quite sweet with the honey and, depending on how sweet your apples are, you may need to adjust further.

Combine all the ingredients in a highball glass and stir gently to combine. Top with ice and garnish with thyme and apple. Drink while you think of your next pun.

Sage

There are a bunch of varieties of sage but, in my opinion, none of them compare to regular old garden sage. Apparently it's quite easy to grow, but it is the one plant I have always had difficulty with. It really shows my purple thumb.

Sage has a rich history in medicinal use. In the past, it was prescribed to treat a range of ailments, from gut issues to excessive perspiration and memory loss. With promises like these, you would have to be silly not to enjoy it daily ... for medicinal purposes, of course.

PLANT
Seeds or plant in spring

GROW
In full sun
Hardy, survives in dry conditions
Deters insects and garden pests
Attracts bees
Companion plant with cabbage and carrots

HARVEST
Pick frequently during spring and autumn for a continuous supply
60–90 days to maturity

Stuffing syrup ⬭

**MAKES APPROX. 300 ML
(10 FL OZ)**

100 g (3½ oz) stale bread,
  roughly torn into small
  pieces
pinch of onion powder
pinch of garlic powder
pinch of salt
100 g (3½ oz) caster
  (superfine) sugar
20 g (¾ oz) sage leaves

Believe it or not, this recipe is probably the one I am most excited about in this book. When Nick and I sat down to look at what we could do for sage, we discussed what we liked about it and looked to food for inspiration. While searching for 'recipes with sage', a stuffing for a roast chicken came up and it reminded me of the stuffing my mum used to make for us kids. I said to Nick, 'Hey, what about a stuffing syrup?' He said 'Get stuffed!' We both laughed and then he said, 'No no, I wasn't joking, that sounds gross'. I convinced him that it was worth trialling, which I did and knocked his socks off with the result. In retrospect, I'm not sure what I liked more, the syrup or proving Nick wrong!

Combine all the ingredients except the sugar and sage in a bowl with 500 ml (17 fl oz/2 cups) water. Leave to sit for 1 hour. Strain, then add the liquid to a saucepan with the sugar and sage. Bring to the boil and simmer for 15 minutes, then strain again and transfer to a sterilised glass bottle (see page 17). The syrup will keep for up to 1 week in the fridge.

For another day

Old fashioned. Use the syrup as the sweetener and grain whisky as the spirit.

French onion dip. Stir through a small amount of syrup to give an extra layer of flavour.

Chicken soup. Use just a little; you don't want a sweet chicken soup.

Sunday roast tea

This little piggy

30 ml (1 fl oz) gin
30 ml (1 fl oz) Stuffing
   syrup (page 185)
90 ml (3 fl oz) fresh
   lemonade (see *Note*)
ice cubes, to garnish
   (optional)
sage sprig, to garnish
   (optional)

Nick named this drink when we were devising the recipes and I made a note to change it once we had finished testing. After testing, I scrubbed out that note with vigour, because this drink makes a person a little piggy; it is incredibly moreish.

Combine all the ingredients in a glass with ice.

Garnish, or don't. After all, the garnish may just get in the way of the drinking.

I would highly recommend making your own lemonade for this recipe. Just mix four parts lemon juice with two parts water and one part Sugar syrup (page 217). However, if that isn't possible, a good-quality, store-bought lemonade (lemon soda) will suffice.

Sunday roast tea

100 ml (3½ fl oz)
   full-cream (whole) milk
2 teaspoons loose-leaf
   black tea
50 ml (1¾ fl oz) Stuffing
   syrup (page 185)

When I was living in the UK, Sundays in winter were my favourite. A group of us would head to the pub to watch the football (the one with the round-shaped ball), drink a few pints and get the roast of the day. After lunch, someone always opted for dessert, and I always opted for tea. There is something about drinking black tea in Britain – it just tastes better. I don't know why. There's no rhyme or reason, but a cup of tea with a splash of milk and no sugar (thank you, I'm not a heathen) is liquid gold. This drink combines these favourite things: Sundays in London, the taste of roasted meat and tea.

Combine the ingredients in a microwave-safe jug and microwave on high (100%) for 1 minute. Remove and stir for 30 seconds. Alternatively, warm in a saucepan over a low heat, stirring occasionally, for around 5 minutes. Strain into a tea cup and chant your favourite team's song.

Nuts

Nuts are such a fantastic way to add body, texture and fats to both foods and drinks. They are high in oil and, when broken down, create an incredible creamy paste.

They are the secret (along with cheese) to making people eat a salad. Learning to cook, I would experiment with different nuts in pesto recipes, fascinated by the different levels of oil and the way they helped to bind the other ingredients.

Then came bartending and fatwashing, which is the process of combining a fat with a liquid to impart flavour, texture and aroma. Once they have been allowed to homogenise, the fats are removed by chilling the liquid until the fats solidify. This process opened the door for combining different nuts with just about every spirit under the sun.

While the nuts featured in this chapter grow in varied climates and countries, they are – like most nuts – harvested in autumn. In this chapter, we look at the nuts that have been washed and dried after harvest. The drying process, where the water content of the nut is reduced to about 8 per cent, makes the nuts stable and accessible year round.

There are plenty of nuts that have not made the chapter: for example, cashews, walnuts, pecans and pine nuts. The ones that did were selected because of their accessibility and connection with beverages. Most nuts, once harvested, will be sent to a processing facility, where the nuts will be mixed with other farm crops. This means that reading labels is very important. Searching out those with organic or biodynamic labels helps. While the produce can't necessarily be traced to an individual producer, it does mean that it is coming from people with like minds and best practices.

—Nick

Hazelnut

The hazelnut is a tree nut, grown in cold climates throughout the world, most prolifically in Turkey, Italy and the USA.

It's popular in an affogato in the form of hazelnut liqueurs such as creme de noisette or Frangelico. But try using them whole, scattered through biscotti and served with coffee.

That said, hazelnuts are most well known for the popularity of two things: Ferrero Rocher chocolates and Nutella chocolate and hazelnut spread. The producer (the same for both) of these popular Italian products is said to use about 25 per cent of the world's annual hazelnut harvest.

Hazelnut honey

**MAKES 500 ML
(17 FL OZ/2 CUPS)**

200 g (7 oz) hazelnuts
400 g (14 oz) light
  wildflower honey
10 g (¼ oz) sea salt
50 ml (1¾ fl oz) brandy

This is a fantastic way to add a savoury edge to honey. The oils give a richness that plays off the light sweetness of the honey. For this reason, a lighter wildflower honey is recommended.

In a saucepan, dry-roast the hazelnuts. Remove from the heat and leave until cool enough to handle, then rub them between your hands to remove the skins.

Roughly blitz the nuts in a food processor, then combine in a saucepan with the honey, sea salt and 50 ml (1¾ fl oz) water. Simmer over a medium heat for 15 minutes. Strain, then combine with the brandy and pour into a sterilised glass bottle (page 15). It is best kept in the fridge for up to 1 month.

For another day

Toast. Mix it with peanut butter for a sweet-and-salty combo.

With your cheese board. All fancy-like.

Toddy. Add a nutty edge to the classic winter hot toddy with a dollop of hazelnut honey.

Espresso noisette

Espresso noisette

45 ml (1½ fl oz)
  cold-brew coffee
  (page 215)
30 ml (1 fl oz) Coconut
  water (page 82)
20 ml (¾ fl oz) Hazelnut
  honey (page 191)
15 ml (½ fl oz) Cacao syrup
  (page 217)
ice cubes, for shaking

A take on the ever-so-popular espresso martini. The blend of nutty elements in the hazelnut, cacao and coconut give all the unadulterated flavour of the original, minus most of the alcohol.

Combine all the ingredients in a shaker and shake hard and fast. You want the coffee to really foam up, giving a velvety texture when strained into a cocktail glass.

Warm cider punch

SERVES 2

330 ml (11 fl oz) dry cider
40 ml (1¼ fl oz) Hazelnut
  honey (page 191)
20 ml (¾ fl oz) herbal
  liqueur
4 dashes of aromatic
  bitters

There is something quite medicinal about a warm cider drink. Maybe it has something to do with the flavours of stewed apples beside a fire. Maybe it is the idea of a warmed apple and cinnamon scroll. (For some reason, everything seems to come back to food with me!) Either way, the combination of fruit, nut honey and spices is an utter delight.

Combine a splash of the cider with the honey in a ceramic jug, stirring to dissolve. Add the liqueur and bitters and zap it in the microwave for 30 seconds. Give it a stir and another 30-second zap. Alternatively, warm in a saucepan over a low heat, stirring occasionally, for around 5 minutes. This is the time to ready your book and beanbag. Pour the cider into two mugs and sip in silence.

Almond

Almonds are the most accessible nuts for me. A tree nut that, interestingly, is part of the same family of fruits as the apricot and plum. When you think about it, this makes sense, as apricot kernels are often substituted for almonds in alcohol production (think amaretto).

The majority of the world's almonds are grown in California's warm climate (many are also grown in Spain and Iran). With such a high number of trees needing pollination, bees are regularly shipped across the country. Because of this, there has been some debate about whether or not almonds are, in fact, vegan. This might sound extreme to some, but we think it really brings home the importance of provenance and learning about how the products you use every day are produced. Always seek out local products made with best practice.

Orgeat ⬦

**MAKES 1.2 LITRES
(41 FL OZ)**

300 g (10½ oz) blanched
  almonds
800 g (1 lb 12 oz) caster
  (superfine) sugar
5 ml (⅛ fl oz)
  orange-blossom water

Orgeat is a classic nut syrup, and forms the backbone of classic cocktails such as the army and navy, and the mai tai. It's one of the most bought syrups, but it's very simple to make and quite luxurious to have fresh.

Blitz the almonds to small chunks in a food processor. Add to a saucepan with 1.5 litres (51 fl oz/6 cups) water and simmer over a medium heat for 30 minutes.

Strain through a piece of muslin (cheesecloth) (see *Note*), then combine the liquid with the sugar and orange-blossom water and stir to dissolve. The orgeat will keep for 2 weeks in the fridge.

Set aside the leftover almond bits from the muslin and dehydrate (see page 14) for use in almond-meal cake.

For another day

Soak cakes. I always enjoyed a citrus syrup on my syrup cakes, until I started bartending and discovered fresh orgeat. Life officially changed.

Ice cream. Top your ice cream with lashings of orgeat.

Make a butter. Combine three parts butter with one part orgeat and roll into a log. Wrap in plastic wrap and rest in the fridge. Serve over anything that needs a hit of nuttiness, like grilled meat or a chocolate brownie for real indulgence.

Mix with lemonade. Or add to an old fashioned for something a bit different.

Nutty frappé

20 ml (¾ fl oz) anise
   liqueur
20 ml (¾ fl oz) Orgeat
   (page 195)
ice cubes, for shaking and
   serving (if needed)
75 ml (2½ fl oz) cola
fresh nutmeg, for grating

An absinthe frappé, for me, was the gateway to liking anise flavours. This is a lighter version, encompassing a lower alcohol, pastis-style anise combined with cola for an afternoon invigorator. One for autumn, when the leaves are starting to fall from the trees and the days are still a little warm, but the evenings are getting chilly.

Combine the anise liqueur and orgeat and shake with ice. Dump into a tall glass and top with cola.

Add more ice if required to fill the glass, then grate a small amount of nutmeg on top.

Nuts & husks ⬡

60 ml (2 fl oz) Iced cascara
   tisane (page 215)
30 ml (1 fl oz) pineapple
   juice
20 ml (¾ fl oz) Orgeat
   (page 195)
2 dashes of Orange bitters
   (page 42)
ice cubes, to serve

Cascara is the husk of the coffee bean. It is often discarded, but makes a fantastic cherry-flavoured tisane. This, with almonds, conjures an almost marasca cherry flavour. Great for a tropical or tiki-style libation to go alongside your daydreams of vacations. Or just have it while you're on vacation.

Combine all the ingredients in a shaker and shake hard. You want the pineapple juice to really fluff up and give the drink a rich head.

Strain into a highball glass and top with ice.

Pistachio

Pistachios should come with a warning that, once you open a bag and sprinkle with salt, you won't be able to stop eating them until you finish the lot. They make a good binding component for any good scroggin mix (trail mix).

The nuts feature heavily in Middle Eastern cuisine, as well as throughout Mediterranean Europe, with some recipes calling for the hard, white shells to be used in the smoking of meats.

When pistachios are fresh, they have an incredible pastel outer skin that can be used for a tisane (see page 214). But this also leaves you with one of the most monotonous tasks in any kitchen: removing the hard, tightly closed shells from the beautiful green nuts.

Pistachio granita

Pistachio granita ◌

SERVES 4

300 g (10½ oz/1⅓ cups)
  raw shelled pistachio
  nuts
200 g (7 oz) caster
  (superfine) sugar
45 ml (1½ fl oz) lemon
  juice
5 ml (⅛ fl oz) rosewater

This is a dish famous for its origins in Sicilian stalls.

In a food processor, blitz the pistachios with 700 ml (25½ fl oz/
3 cups) water. Pour the mixture into a saucepan and simmer over
a medium-low heat for 15 minutes. Strain the liquid and stir in
the sugar until dissolved.

Add the remaining ingredients, then pour into a baking tray and
freeze. After 45 minutes, remove the tray from the freezer and
use a fork to scrape frozen shards of granita. Repeat this process
three times, then freeze for another 2 hours before using a fork
to scrape the granita into a fluffy mix.

Once frozen, the granita will keep for 1 month. However, the
longer it is frozen the harder it will be to rough up.

For another day

Serve with brioche. Do like the Italians do, or just eat it out of the
baking tray.

Lift it. Add some pistachio granita to a G&T or vodka soda for an
interesting lift.

Whisked away 💧

35 ml (1¼ fl oz)
  gin-flavoured hydrosol
  (see page 11)
2 tablespoons Pistachio
  granita (opposite)
20 ml (¾ fl oz) Mint-stem
  cordial (page 173)

I was once given a demonstration of how to make a matcha tea. This cocktail takes inspiration from the process of using a wooden whisk to gently combine the matcha tea with water. Incidentally, the vibrant green colour of the matcha pairs perfectly with the pistachio granita.

This drink also uses a gin hydrosol, a non-alcoholic distilled beverage that contains all the botanical components of a gin without the alcohol. Often, hydrosols are quite lacklustre when tasted on their own but, once diluted, their flavour can really bolster a drink.

Combine all the ingredients in a ceramic cup and whisk gently with a tea whisk. You will feel as though you are partaking in a traditional tea ceremony.

Stepping on shells

30 ml (1 fl oz) white rum
2 tablespoons Pistachio
  granita (opposite)
20 ml (¾ fl oz) verjus
  (see page 218)
5 ml (⅛ fl oz) grenadine
  (page 219)
3 lemon balm sprigs,
  to garnish

When I was younger, I would sit at a table outside with my siblings, devouring pistachios. None of the shells would make it into the scraps bowl. They would all be on the floor. This was a mistake, as stepping on the shells was akin to stepping on Lego blocks – painful, and incredibly annoying. This is where the name for this cocktail comes from.

Combine all the ingredients except the lemon balm in a shaker and shake sharp and fast. Dump it all into a large rocks glass and garnish with the lemon balm for a fresh, aromatic finish.

Macadamia

Macadamias are a tropical rainforest nut. They are native to Australia but have spread around tropical parts of the world. Very high in oils and rich in flavour with a soft flesh, they have been the jewel in the crown of Australian native exports for a long time. Throughout the eighties and nineties, Hawaii cultivated and made an international name for the nuts and, as a result, growing regions expanded around the world. Besides Australia, macadamias are most prolifically grown in South Africa and Brazil.

Macadamia milk

**MAKES 1 LITRE
(34 FL OZ/4 CUPS)**

**200 g (7 oz/1¼ cups)
macadamia nuts**

This is a base recipe that works well with most nuts to make a dairy-free, creamy liquid that is very versatile for both breakfast dishes and your morning coffee. If you are feeling adventurous, you can also incorporate a touch of spice in the blitzing process, but I prefer to keep it simple and adjust when making drinks later on.

In a food processor, blitz the macadamia nuts with 1 litre (34 fl oz/4 cups) water. Allow to sit for 30 minutes before straining through a piece of muslin (cheesecloth). The milk will keep in the fridge in an airtight container for up to 1 week.

Reserve the macadamia meal, dry it out and use it to add texture to cereal or in a crumble topping.

For another day

Coffee. Use it as a milk substitute in hot or iced coffee.

For cereal. Shaun likes Nutri-Grain.

Hinterland range

Hinterland range

60 ml (2 fl oz) Macadamia
milk (page 203)
30 ml (1 fl oz) Peach
liqueur (page 99)
1 egg yolk
2 ml (⅛ fl oz) orange-
blossom water
2 dashes aromatic bitters
ice cubes, for shaking and
serving
30 ml (1 fl oz) soda water
(club soda)

For me, macadamias are always about the picturesque drive into
the northern rivers hinterland above Byron Bay in New South
Wales. It's a tropical haven of growth, with roadside market stalls
full of produce from local growers. The colour of this drink will
remind you of the sun starting to rise over the eastern sea horizon,
shining in the rear-view mirror as you drive up the hill.

Combine all the ingredients except the soda water in a shaker,
then shake aggressively, making sure the egg yolk is well whipped
through.

Strain into a goblet, add a splash of soda and top with ice.

Northern migration 💧

60 ml (2 fl oz) Macadamia
milk (page 203)
60 ml (2 fl oz) cold-brew
coffee (page 215)
20 ml (¾ fl oz) condensed
milk
dash of aromatic bitters
ice cubes, to serve

Taking inspiration from a Vietnamese iced coffee, this is a rich and
sweet pick-me-up. Although often seen served in a plastic bag at
a market stall, I think it is refined enough to deserve a fancy glass.

Combine all the ingredients in a glass and stir to combine, then
top with ice.

Alternatively, make a batch of five at a time and store in a glass
jar in the fridge. In times of need, just shake and pour a generous
helping over ice.

Peanut

Peanuts cop a bad rap. They are nutritious morsels, but are often avoided due to fear of allergic reactions. There are a number of theories as to why peanuts in particular cause such reactions. Firstly, peanut oil is used frequently in infant creams. Secondly, in the age of clean eating, people are cutting out more and more 'allergens' and, in the process, creating sensitivities to certain ingredients.

Peanuts are not actually nuts but part of the legume family. They grow on a small plant that flowers above ground, then drops vines where the peanuts grow below ground. They thrive in hot, dry climates, particularly in China, India and Nigeria.

Salted peanut water ⬦

MAKES 800 ML
(27 FL OZ)

300 g (10½ oz) raw
  peanuts
100 g (3½ oz) caster
  (superfine) sugar
10 g (¼ oz) salt

This recipe was created to make a cocktail for a travelling American chef. We wanted to make a salty, low-sugar base for a rocky road cocktail, to be served alongside his ice creams.

Dry-roast the peanuts in a saucepan for 5 minutes over a medium heat. Combine with the rest of the ingredients and 1.5 litres (51 fl oz/6 cups) water in a saucepan and simmer for 30 minutes.

Strain the water through a piece of muslin (cheesecloth), then pour into a sterilised glass bottle (see page 15) and refrigerate for up to 1 week.

For another day

Cook bananas in it. Then serve it with ice cream.

Use as the base of a satay sauce. Just add coconut cream and chilli paste.

Sweet-stall memories

30 ml (1 fl oz) Salted
  peanut water (page 207)
20 ml (¾ fl oz) grain whisky
20 ml (¾ fl oz) curaçao
20 ml (¾ fl oz) Coconut
  water (page 82)
10 ml (¼ fl oz) Sugar syrup
  (page 217)
2 dashes of aromatic
  bitters
1 egg white
ice cubes, for shaking
raspberry lollies (sweets),
  to serve (optional)

At every school fête I went to there was a mother selling rocky road at a sweet stall. My mother ran that stall for quite a number of years. It certainly wasn't my favourite sweet, or the best made, but its playfulness made it popular. This cocktail has all the components of this sweet, without the chocolate. Instead, that element comes through in the whisky.

Combine all the ingredients except the ice and raspberry lollies in a shaker and dry-shake vigorously to combine the egg whites. Add ice and shake again.

Strain into a cocktail glass and serve with a side of raspberry lollies to complete the rocky road theme.

Rocky brew 💧

70 ml (2¼ fl oz) cold-brew
  coffee (page 215)
30 ml (1 fl oz) Salted
  peanut water (page 207)
20 ml (¾ fl oz) Cacao syrup
  (page 217)
ice cubes, to serve

I don't know about everyone else, but I need my coffee to function. It is such a staple part of my day. That is why I like to vary it. This is another drink that I like to batch and drink at the end of a long afternoon before heading to the bar for work.

Combine all the ingredients in a glass. Stir to combine, then top with ice. It's that easy!

Basics

The recipes in this chapter are staples that Nick and I have used over the years in countless drinks. They are the hard-working, blue-collar recipes. They are the recipes that are easily forgotten, as they usually don't take the limelight, but are necessary all the same. Most of them are incredibly straightforward and all of them have uses beyond the pages of this book.

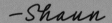

—Shaun

Juice

Many drinks call for juice and, while it may seem quite simple to make, there are a few tricks to ensuring you get the juiciest juice you can possibly juice.

Orange, lemon, lime & yuzu (well, all citrus, really)

If you can get unwaxed citrus, then this is certainly the best way to go. Look to organic produce and farmers for this, or your neighbour's tree.

There are a couple of other key points to consider when juicing citrus, and the first is the zest. The zest contains intensely aromatic oils that have quite a number of uses. Peeling your citrus fruit and combining it with sugar (even salt) will give you a fragrant product that can be used on any number of dishes. To extract citrus juice, I recommend using a manual juicer as the electric ones may introduce a bit of heat to the juice, which detracts from the flavour and freshness. It's also good to find a juicer that puts some pressure on the fruit – one with a handle you pull down. This helps release the oils from the zest (if you haven't already removed it), giving you a more fragrant juice. You can also get hand-held juicers for making drinks on the go.

Fennel

Fennel does best when juiced using a centrifugal juicer (see page 13). Take the bulb, and remove the stalks and fronds to use later. Cut the brown base off and chop the bulb into small enough pieces to put into your juicer.

Ginger

One of my favourites. I think the first recipe I developed for Gin Palace was a ginger beer syrup with fresh ginger and lime juice with sugar. You want to obtain ginger as young as possible, as the older it gets (you can tell, as the skin gets increasingly brown and flaky) the spicier it gets. Whether young or old, it's best to peel it; it can be a bit fiddly, but it yields better results and is better for your juicer. Chop your ginger into small cubes, around 2–4 cm (¾–1½ in), and feed it into your centrifugal juicer.

Pineapple

To select your pineapple for juicing, just smell the fruit. If it smells fresh and vibrant, it's good to go. If the aroma is a little deeper with a slight funk, then I would avoid it. Remove the skin and core, then juice away. Best done in a centrifugal juicer.

Cucumber

As I am sure you have seen in the aisles of your local supermarket, cucumbers are often individually wrapped in plastic (well, some of the more thin-skinned varieties are anyway). This apparently makes them last longer. For my two bobs worth, I think it's a bit wasteful. If my cucumbers start to turn, I just eat them and, as they are mostly water, I always feel refreshed. If you must buy the plastic-wrapped ones, be sure to give them a bit of a rinse after you've unwrapped them. Firm cucumbers are the best to work with; no need to skin them, just chop them into smaller pieces before popping into your centrifugal juicer.

Apple

As with citrus, get your apples unwaxed if possible and, once again, organic farmers' markets and your neighbour's tree are your best bet here. Something really off-putting about apples is when the waxed ones have been left out for too long in warmer temperatures and they look really shiny. It's not appealing at all. For juicing, make sure your apple is firm. Chuck it into the centrifugal juicer whole (or cut into smaller pieces if need be), no peeling required, and don't worry about removing the pips.

Teas, tisanes & coffees ◊

I love tea. It's my go-to when I am avoiding alcohol, and I drink it hot in the winter and cold in the summer. As I'm from Melbourne, coffee is also a staple and I am partial to a cup of mint tea every now and then. Here, we have a bunch of recipes for teas, tisanes and coffees.

Black tea

This is what I grew up on, as mum used to love making cups of tea for us when we were kids. Local to me in Australia is some great tea from the Daintree region in Queensland. Further afield, I like Darjeeling the most, but am also partial to a lapsang souchong in the middle of winter. Keep your black tea (all tea, actually) in an airtight container away from direct light.

Type	Qty tea	Qty water & temp	Qty sugar	Brew time	Makes approx.
Hot	10 g (¼ oz)	500 ml (17 fl oz/2 cups) & 100°C (210°F)	0 g	3 minutes	Tea for 2
Iced/cold-brew	50 g (1¾ oz)	1 litre (34 fl oz/4 cups) & chilled	50 g (1¾ oz)	12 hours in the fridge	900 ml (30½ fl oz)
Syrup	40 g (1½ oz)	800 ml (27 fl oz) & 100°C (210°F)	400 g (14 oz)	8 minutes	1 litre (34 fl oz/ 4 cups)

Green tea

There is a tea grower in north-eastern Victoria called Perfect South. I really like their shinsha, which is the first harvest of a Japanese-style green tea, so it's nutty and stone-fruity all at the same time.

Type	Qty tea	Qty water & temp	Qty sugar	Brew time	Makes approx.
Hot	5 g (⅙ oz)	500 ml (17 fl oz/2 cups) & 75°C (167°F)	0 g	2 minutes	Tea for 2
Iced/cold-brew	35 g (1¼ oz)	1 litre (34 fl oz/4 cups) & chilled	50 g (1¾ oz)	12 hours in the fridge	800 ml (27 fl oz)
Syrup	25 g (1 oz)	800 ml (27 fl oz) & 75°C (167°F)	300 g (10½ oz)	10 minutes	1 litre (34 fl oz/ 4 cups)

Mint

A hot mint tea when it's still warm outside goes down a treat. I'm not sure how that works (hot liquid during hot weather), but it does! There isn't a syrup recipe here, as you'll find one on page 173. Lastly, when working with mint, use the stems and the leaves.

Type	Qty mint	Qty water & temp	Qty sugar	Brew time	Makes approx.
Hot	10 g (¼ oz)	500 ml (17 fl oz/2 cups) & 75°C (167°F)	0 g	2 minutes	Tea for 2
Iced/cold-brew	100 g (3½ oz)	1 litre (34 fl oz/4 cups) & chilled	0 g	12 hours in the fridge	1 litre (34 fl oz/ 4 cups)

Cascara

I remember reading once that coffee is the third most consumed beverage in the world. The same cannot be said for the byproduct of coffee: cascara. Cascara is the husk of the coffee cherry and, when dried, it makes a delightful tisane, kind of cherry-like in flavour.

Type	Qty cascara	Qty water & temp	Qty sugar	Brew time	Makes approx.
Hot	10 g (¼ oz)	500 ml (17 fl oz/2 cups) & 100°C (210°F)	0 g	3 minutes	Tea for 2
Iced/cold-brew	50 g (1¾ oz)	1 litre (34 fl oz/4 cups) & chilled	50 g (1¾ oz)	12 hours in the fridge	1 litre (34 fl oz/ 4 cups)
Syrup	40 g (1½ oz)	800 ml (27 fl oz) & 100°C (210°F)	300 g (10½ oz)	10 minutes	1 litre (34 fl oz/ 4 cups)

Coffee

The trick with coffee is to use it as freshly roasted and, more importantly, as freshly ground as possible. The terroir of coffee also affects the flavour (similar to grapes in wine), as does temperature, with more bitter flavours coming out at higher temperatures.

Type	Qty coffee	Qty water & temp	Qty sugar	Brew time	Makes approx.
Hot	25 g (1 oz)	500 ml (17 fl oz/2 cups) & 100°C (210°F)	0 g	3 minutes	Coffee for 2
Iced/cold-brew	70 g (2½ oz)	1 litre (34 fl oz/4 cups) & chilled	0 g	12 hours in the fridge	800 ml (27 fl oz)
Syrup	100 g (3½ oz)	1 litre (34 fl oz/4 cups) & chilled	500 g (1 lb 2 oz)	12 hours in the fridge	1 litre (34 fl oz/ 4 cups)

Adjusting solutions & syrups 💧

Salt and pepper in the kitchen are much the same as these adjusting solutions behind the bar. If a cocktail tastes imbalanced, it can often be rectified by including one of the following recipes in a small proportion.

Solutions

Citric solution

A great correcting solution when citrus isn't in season and you need to get a little more acid into your beverage. To make, simply dissolve one part citric acid in five parts water. There is no need for heat here. You can also experiment with different types of acid, such as tartaric (from grapes) and malic (from apples) for different effects.

Saline solution

Potatoes aren't potatoes without a little salt. Salt has a magical power to just make things taste better – in the right quantities, that is. To make a saline solution, simply dissolve one part salt in five parts water, no heat required. Flaked salt is best here, and there is a world of salt varieties to experiment with.

Syrups

Sugar syrup

Probably the most common of all the adjusting solutions, sugar syrup is a great way to help carry flavour. I always opt for a two parts sugar to one part water concentration instead of the popular equal parts solution. The reason is that you don't want to add unnecessary water to your cocktail, or at least not in most circumstances. To make a sugar syrup, simply dissolve two parts sugar in one part water in a saucepan over a gentle heat. Caster (superfine) sugar works best here, but you can experiment with different sugars, such as brown or fructose, for different effects.

Spiced syrup

Spicing a sugar syrup is a really easy way to get solid flavour in a liquid form. These recipes are all very straightforward and can be accomplished with minimal fuss. All the recipes below will make around 500 ml (17 fl oz/2 cups) of syrup.

Item	Amount	Water	Sugar	Citric acid	Cook time
Cacao	20 g (¾ oz) nibs	400 ml (13½ fl oz)	450 g (1 lb)	0 g	Simmer for 1 hour
Elderflower	10 g (¼ oz) fresh or 5 g (⅛ oz) dried	400 ml (13½ fl oz)	350 g (12½ oz)	5 g (⅛ oz)	Simmer for 30 minutes
Kaffir lime leaf	10 g (¼ oz), torn	400 ml (13½ fl oz)	350 g (12½ oz)	0 g	Simmer for 30 minutes
Lemongrass	1 stalk, muddled	400 ml (13½ fl oz)	350 g (12½ oz)	5 g (⅛ oz)	Simmer for 30 minutes
Oak	20 g (¾ oz) oak chips	400 ml (13½ fl oz)	250 g (9 oz)	0 g	Simmer for 30 minutes
Vanilla	1 bean, halved and scraped	400 ml (13½ fl oz)	150 g (5½ oz)	0 g	Simmer for 1 hour

Bar essentials ⬦

These are the staples of the staples. I always have a bottle of each of these in my fridge and have to top them up frequently. Sometimes I make these recipes and sometimes I buy the ones that are commercially available. It all depends on how busy I am writing books!

Verjus

This is something I have never made, which is a bit embarrassing, as I have quite a lot of access to grapes. Verjus is essentially unripe grape juice. It acts as a very light vinegar and is wonderful in beverages. Nick and I are quite fond of it as you will no doubt notice in this book. You can get white verjus, red verjus and even the named grape variety for the more premium ones. Buy a couple, experiment, find your favourite, and then look for some more.

Honey syrup

The variety of honeys available is vast, and the flavour changes depending on the location and where the bees are spending their time. Honey can be a bit difficult to work with in drinks, as it can be sticky and create quite a mess, so I usually work the honey into a syrup first. This can be very easily achieved by combining one part warm water with two parts honey. Stir until the consistency is runny. Be sure to keep it in the fridge, as you don't want it turning to mead – or do you?

Tonic syrup

I must preface this by saying that working with cinchona bark can be dangerous; if you extract too much quinine it can cause cinchonism or quinine toxicity, so please don't imbibe too much syrup. The recipe below is what I use at home and is very easy to make. However, there are some great commercial brands out there as well, so if you are time poor explore those options instead.

Combine all the ingredients except the sugar in a saucepan with 750 ml (25½ fl oz/3 cups) water. Bring to the boil and simmer for 30 minutes.

Strain the liquid into the sugar through a coffee filter, paper towel or clean, disposable cloth, then stir until the sugar has dissolved. Transfer to a sterilised glass bottle (see page 15) and store in the fridge for up to 2 months.

Find cinchona bark powder online from speciality suppliers.

**MAKES 500 ML
(17 FL OZ/2 CUPS)**

5 g (⅛ oz) coriander seed
5 g (⅛ oz) angelica root
5 g (⅛ oz) citric acid
2 g (⅟₁₆ oz) cinchona bark
   powder (see *Note*)
pinch of sea salt
300 g (10½ oz) caster
   (superfine) sugar

Grenadine

The word grenadine comes from the French word for pomegranate, *grenade*, so it should come as no surprise that grenadine is a pomegranate syrup. However, you could be forgiven for mistaking it if you have tasted commercially produced grenadines, which to me are no more than red sugar water. Luckily there are some great smaller brands producing quality grenadine now. If it is the season for pomegranates, why not try making a well-made, hand-crafted one of your own?

Juice the pomegranates using a manual juicer, similar to how you would juice citrus (see page 212). You should have around 350 ml (12 fl oz) of juice. If you have more, drink it; if you have less, drop the sugar to equal parts.

Combine the remaining ingredients with the pomegranate juice and dissolve the sugar with vigorous stirring (or use a hand-held blender). It will last for up to 1 month in the fridge.

**MAKES APPROX. 500 ML
(17 FL OZ/2 CUPS)**

3 pomegranates
350 g (12½ oz) caster
   (superfine) sugar
30 ml (1 fl oz) pomegranate
   molasses
dash of orange-blossom
   water

Index

Italicised entries indicate no-alcohol recipes.

About the authors

Shaun and Nick started working together at Melbourne's Gin Palace in January 2013. Since those early days, they have always worked closely.

Shaun moved on from Gin Palace to spend more time on his vermouth company Maidenii, which he co-founded in 2011 with winemaker Gilles Lapalus. At Maidenii in Central Victoria, the focus is on using native botanicals, quality wine and local produce to craft vermouth. Shaun also started a consulting company called Good Measure, which focuses on events and education in the liquor industry, with more of a focus on sustainability the older he gets.

Nick went on to be part of the opening team at the wildly creative Restaurant Lûmé in South Melbourne, where he was responsible for beverage recipe development. Here, Nick says, he 'focused on getting the most out of incredible Australian produce, thinking laterally to extract flavour using the best equipment available'. After an eighteen-month stint, he moved on to splitting his time between Bad Frankie, an Australian-only spirits bar and Bar Liberty, a prominent wine bar that eventually got named Wine Bar of the Year at the Australian Bartender Awards.

In 2017 Nick and Shaun started Marionette Liqueurs with a couple of mates, Lauren Bonkowski and Hugh Leech. They all saw a gap in the market for premium-quality, locally produced liqueurs and were shocked at the lack of supply given the quality of produce available in Australia. Their mission is to work directly with Australian farmers to produce cocktail staples (such as cassis, curaçao and mure, to name a few) needed for mixing fine drinks.

Thank you

To Hugh, Lauren and Gilles, our business partners in Marionette and Maidenii. Thanks for your support and for covering workload to make the writing of this book possible.

For their help and guidance with the sustainability chapter, Brendan Carter (Applewood Distillery), Sebastian Costello (Bad Frankie), Sebastian Raeburn and Dervilla McGowan (Anther Gin). Thank you for the wise words and for being such solid sounding boards.

Richard Clark (Westerway Raspberry Farm), John Mantovani (Manto Produce), Glen Goldup (Goldup Farms) and Jimmy Ripepi (Australian Strawberry Distributors), our Marionette farmers. Our relationships with you over the past couple of years have taught us a lot.

Liam, of Spurrell Foraging, we appreciate you teaching us all how to better grow herbs at home.

To our families, for shaping our love of food and passion for produce. Heather and Peter, Nola and CJ, thank you. Olive (Grandma), thank you for your recipes (the ones that I could understand). To Shaun's wife, Ellen, thanks for allowing us the space to make such a mess of your kitchen, but also for making Shaun more balanced.

Our talented friends in kitchens, who allow us to lean on their experience: Mike Layfield, Vicky Symington and Casey Wall, your assistance is invaluable. John Tripoldi, Charlie Di Stasi, Katie Finlay, we appreciate you being our personal market guides to seasonality.

Michael and Banjo at Bar Liberty and Capitano – for the use of your spaces, but also for keeping Nick employed.

Thanks to all the bartenders, past and present, who we have listened to over the years. In particular, the creative weapons that are Andy Griffiths, James Whittington, Orlando Marzo, Trish Brew, Darren Leaney, James Connolly and Zeb Platter. Thank you to the authors of the many, many books we read while developing this book (you can find a full list of our references at marionette.com.au/alldaycocktails).

Finally, the team at Hardie Grant, in particular Jane, Loran and Andrea; you have been incredibly patient and your guidance has been immaculate. And the creative team of Jessica, Vanessa, Stephanie and Gavin, we love your work.